Notes After Midnight

Notes After Midnight

How I Outlasted My Teenagers,
One Mistake at a Time

Carol Richmond

SHE WRITES PRESS

Published September 2019
Printed in the United States of America
Print ISBN: 978-1-63152-633-6
E-ISBN: 978-1-63152-632-9
Library of Congress Control Number: 2019906678

For information, address:
She Writes Press
1569 Solano Ave #546
Berkeley, CA 94707

Interior design by Tabitha Lahr

She Writes Press is a division of SparkPoint Studio, LLC.

Ashton, Scooter, and Cinnamon:
Thank you for sharing the path of your lives with me

"Best not to begin. Once begun, best to finish."
—*Anonymous*

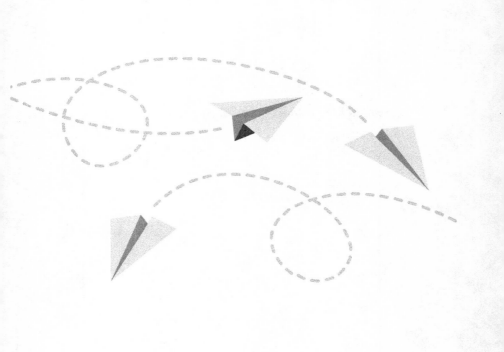

Introduction

My destiny as the child of older parents, like that of any child within a family, was guided by fate. In the era during which I was raised, children beget by old maids and widowers usually arrived with a slew of potential problems. By all rights, I should have been born a cabbage. Considering the average age of first-time mothers in the mid-1950s was 22.8 years old, a forty-five year-old mother and fifty-five-year-old father were the exception and far from the rule.

And so, I landed in a home with two mismatched humans attempting to be happy. My father loved camping, the outdoors, and puns. My mother likened camping to a hotel without room service. She couldn't understand why anyone would bother making reservations, much less checking in. On this subject, I am my mother's daughter.

A single widower and an old maid, Mr. Outdoors met Miss Pampered, and they lived happily ever after. Well, if you count the fact that I was the sole reason for the happily ever after. My mother invested her dreams, desires, and warped sense of an ideal relationship in me at an early age. When conflict arose, my father simply left the house and took a good long walk. That worked for him but left me to my own devices with her. There was no question, even at a young age, that I had been misplaced with this family. Since I am a rebel, I spent a goodly portion of my time proving I was right. My father was a gentle man. Once, when Mother told him I had been naughty as a four-year-old and certainly deserved a spanking, he took me into the bathroom, clapped his hands, and told me to scream. In contrast, as a preteen know-it-all and after a sassy retort to my mother, my punishment from her was to kneel in front of a heating vent and pray continuously out loud for forgiveness, as she listened in the basement while she ironed on a contraption called a mangle.

In 1956, impulsive children were leashed to their parent or caregiver, and, being a prime flight risk and rebel, I earned my mother's worry and a short tether at two years old. I could usually be found, however, near shiny objects in the jewelry cases at the local department store should I wriggle free while she was trying on shoes. My quest for freedom grew, along with persistent talk of wishing I had been born the opposite sex. My line of reasoning did nothing to quell her fears, and my consistent gender questioning really sent her over the edge. I desperately wanted to be a boy. This so worried my mother that I was immediately hauled to a psychologist to figure out how to fix my problem. I was six years old when this started. For me, this desire wasn't so much about rejecting my gender as it was about envying the freedom and rights I saw in the neighborhood boys. Boys didn't have to stay close to the house; they could play fearlessly until after dark; and I found most intriguing and irritating their code of exclusion, especially of girls. Did I want to play baseball? No. Did I care a lick about Red Rover? No. What got my ire was the subtle suggestion that I was inferior.

Apparently unaffected by my desire to have more freedom, my father simply abdicated child-rearing duties to my mother. As the boss of the house, my mother was a feminist with her own platform. After her father died, she was left the sole owner of a lumber company in southwestern Michigan, and she ran a tight ship. I don't remember ever seeing her cower, be it before a yard foreman or any other authority. If she believed she was right—and that was all the time—she would fight to be right. If the job wasn't done to her satisfaction, you were to move over and let Rosie do it. She, too, was the only child of older parents, and many times she exhibited the more negative traits of this stereotype: spoiled, egotistical, and self-serving. If you were on her good side, the world was calm, but a storm could be brewing and hit land before you felt the wind pick up. Most of the time, I strived to be on her good side.

My father, Jack, was not a fighter. He left life to its course and attempted to fit in. In my recollection, he didn't raise his voice or deny my mother's decisions, and his steadfast constitution carried the belief that everything would work out if you stayed calm and rational. He didn't give a fig about my boy phase. As the eldest of ten children whose mother had died in childbirth when he was fifteen, he was inclined to ignore outbursts and attempt to make peace. His stepmother kicked him out of the house at sixteen, and, though he never appeared to have been affected, he also never spoke about those times. His wounds were too deep to penetrate his thinking, so he simply ignored them. He was a gentle man and a gentleman. He gave back through his fraternal organizations and was generous with his time and resources. It was a marriage of opposites.

As my father aged, his ailments worsened, and he searched for a perfect climate to control his health issues. At the time, the moniker COPD ("chronic obstructive pulmonary disease") was in an exploratory pulmonary rehabilitation phase. In the beginning of his search for a respiratory respite, he would leave at the first snowfall and return in the spring. After three Michigan winters alone, my mother was done running her family's company business, a lumberyard and general hardware store, and done being on her own for so long—and possibly for so long alone with me. After that, his winter travels became a family affair as we trekked around the United States, living together a winter here and a year there—south Florida for a winter, Mississippi for a winter, Louisiana for a year, and finally settling in South Texas in an attempt to find a space where the poor man could take a deep breath.

The year I was nine, we landed in a small Louisiana parish complete with hardcore racism. Having spent years in the North, I hadn't known there was such tension. I hadn't been raised around many people of color. There were Negros (the correct term at the time) where I was born, but there was not socialization across colors. If there was contact, it was because they were cleaning your house or, in our case, working in the lumberyard for my mother. Schools were yet to be totally integrated. Why there were a couple of Negro children in the backwoods Louisiana parish school where I ended up was never explained. It must have been hell for the black children to be so few among so many white children. Whites on the inside of society automatically inferred acceptance, while blacks on the outside of accepted society were just that—out. I was on the inside of acceptance; I just didn't know it, didn't understand it, and didn't believe it.

I was deeply touched by the insidious thread of injustice exhibited in the classroom and on the playground, though I could neither explain my bubbling wrath nor spell the word *injustice*. I knew there was something radically wrong, and, true to my form, whenever I had enough the world became quickly aware. The playground bullying, ill-equipped classrooms, brokenhearted teachers exhausted from the daily fight to educate kids who have been pushed on without grade level skills, and heads continually turned from blatant inappropriate remarks, all thrown in the pot and left unchecked, resulted in daily fights that the teachers and administration pretended not to notice. They didn't have the skills to help or the global vision to change what could be changed.

My mother, having been raised in the South, took no notice of my stories regarding racial inequality; after all, she understood the Southern hierarchy with her childhood history of upstairs help, downstairs help, a cook, and a driver. In third grade, I punched a fellow classmate in the left eye because he hated "n-ggers." I didn't understand why I got suspended and he didn't. I knew what he was saying, and the way he hurled insults was unacceptable. Unconventional humanitarian meets 1960s Southern Louisiana. With some promises of good behavior, I was admitted back to the third grade to finish the year. It was made quite clear I should be gracious about the leniency, and yet even with my mother's mea culpas, I had been branded a troublemaker. I didn't make any lasting friends, and we moved again after that school year.

Each one of us bears the scars of parenting, whether it comes from our parents or from ourselves as parents and what we have pompously or piously bestowed on our progeny. No one is immune. If they say they had a perfect childhood, they lie, or they came of age in the '60s and simply cannot remember. You might laugh at the loss of memory, yet a few years back I attempted to reunite on Facebook with a former elementary school classmate, now a trial attorney on the East Coast. We had played together in the neighborhood. One Christmas, Eddie had unceremoniously broken my new life-size play oven. I punched him in the eye, and he ran crying home. (I might seem to have a pattern of violence, yet I can assure anyone reading, this and the boy in the last section are the only two males I have ever struck—for good reason and not that there shouldn't have been more.) I reached out to Eddie these fifty years later to commiserate about aging and to laugh at the memory, yet he did not remember the episode. He advised me to call his ninety-eight-year-old mother, as she had a better recollection of life's events. I did not call.

My parents' brand of child-rearing coupled with my inherent mercurial, impetuous, and spontaneous personality would lead me on a search for the mate who would give me what I was lacking: stability, unconditional love, economic security, adoration, forever love—you get the warped picture. I was seeking a knight in shining armor. My mother always said I was searching for the "limelight," when it was her vision I sought to uncover.

My mother had a colloquialism for every possible event. The term *limelight* was coined in the 1820s by Goldsworth Gurney, chemistry and philosophy lecturer and part-time inventor, who found that introducing a small chunk of lime (the stone, not the fruit) to a flame resulted in a blinding white light that could be visible for miles. Mom had a point, yet I didn't see myself as a would-be limelight actress; I didn't see anything. I just was being—reacting to what was put in front of me. Planning wasn't something that interested me. I went from one circumstance to the next, accepting and adjusting, praying for something to save me when I should have been saving myself. That lesson would take the better part of six decades to learn.

What I got was a life of noise, a lack of privacy and personal space, a first husband with four ex-wives and three stepchildren, and a loss of youth and of who I was and what I might have wanted had I thought through anything but the present moment. I thought I wanted what I got, but I can't say for certain that I did.

I freely admit I would do it all differently if there were do-overs. Even with the thought of different marriage and children, I would have waited on the blind acceptance and harsh reality of marriage at nineteen. Travel should have been a priority in the late 1960s and 1970s, when I was coming into adulthood and the global experience was still mystifying. I lacked the courage to do what I wanted to do, instead of fruitlessly attempting to please someone else, whether that goal was real or imagined. Safety was the only route I could visualize, and, with that ingrained mindset, I didn't see I had options.

Fortunately, my mother gifted me with travel and sent me on a three-month, multi-country European jaunt the summer before my last year of high school. It was a VW tour bus entourage filled with young college men and women led by two handsome, young, college frat brothers—and me, one high school senior. A growth experience, Mother called it. She pushed me out of the nest, but this came with a caveat—my prince would come on a white horse to save me, and soon. I was instructed to keep my eyes open and be a good girl, should I have the fortune of meeting an eligible bachelor. Mixed messages were abundant living with Rosie.

I chose safety in marriage at nineteen to John. He was days shy of his fiftieth birthday, and you cannot have a relationship with a man thirty years your senior without a trainload of baggage. His baggage consisted of three children, two under the age of ten—a boy and a girl—and one seventeen-year-old boy, just two years younger than me. Four marriages had produced two sets of offspring.

The first of our own three children would not arrive for seven years. Until then, I raised his two younger ones. The nine-year-old-boy was picked up every Friday after school and delivered back to his mother on Sunday night. The ten-year-old daughter moved in with us immediately after we were married. The mother of the two children was ill-equipped to handle the typical emotional outbursts of her preteen daughter and simply said, "You take her, I can't handle her." The boy was easier, and she didn't want to relinquish both children for fear of John withholding child support. Her compromise freed her weekends to pursue a new life and love without hindrance.

My life became a marathon of children's afterschool lessons, grocery shopping at big box store behemoths, work, weekend evening black-tie events, and . . . well, you get the picture. No time to stop and reflect because that would mean I would have to stop and reflect. Way too scary.

It would take years before I realized that the man who'd become father to my own three children would never allow me to grow or change. There were frequent judgmental comments that led to threats of his suicide should I leave the marriage. My oldest was eight before I realized I was done and there was no way other than straight out the nearest door. It was time to go it alone.

When I say alone, there were countless people who were there—helpers, those who listened, those who didn't listen, and those who wanted more and less from a single mother with three children. But I was alone in my heart and in my head, raising children as the lone decision maker, provider, psychologist, pet sitter, grievance manager, and all the things two parents usually are together.

It was ten years before I married again. The children began the normal process of leaving home, one by one, to pursue their passions and to flee the confines of questioning, prodding, and take-out-the-trash requests. Everything came to an end—the endless dinner party circuit, the charity events, the hours of full-time motherhood. It was all just as well. After all, wasn't I tired of seeing the same people at the same events with the same fake smiles, all of us wishing we were home in our jammies with a straw in the wine bottle? It couldn't just be my fantasy.

This story stems from those times, and it isn't a fantasy. It's based on reflective notes written by my children on Post-its, envelopes, and scraps of odd papers, which I found in a shoebox while packing forty years of life in the flurry of a move. I sat on the floor by the box and looked at the over two hundred scraps of our lives, and a flood of memories rushed into my mind. I don't remember how I survived those years, yet at that moment, I knew there was a story to tell that would, perhaps, inspire another mother to persevere.

Notes after Midnight is the story of listening to my intuition, rising to the consequences created by my decisions, and doing the best I could at the time with what I had created. It is a story of trust when I didn't believe, confidence when it would have been easier to run the other way, and forgiving myself for not having the right answers all the time—or even most of the time. Writing this book has given me a retrospective outlook on what was an incredibly difficult and pivotal eight-year timeframe as a single parent, starting when my youngest was two and my oldest eight. *Notes after Midnight* covers the later years. It was the boys who started it, especially Ashton at age fifteen, and I would see looking back at these notes that life is what you make it.

It really is a choice of being happy where you are in the moment, laughing after a good cry, and trusting the Universe however the perception of your belief system operates. There are no promises, yet living and loving make the human species feel alive, boundless, and able to conquer difficulties. Most of the time we are so deep in the weeds that we cannot see above, or we succumb to fear as it creeps, cascading its dark cloak around our shoulder. If we can conquer fear, freedom awaits with open arms. Alas, this concept is fleeting.

Danger and mayhem, I am unashamed to admit, were alive and well in our one-parent home. Why anyone would want to enter that zone, I don't know, yet I am grateful he did. He is called Reg in this missive, and he partnered with me in raising my three children for twenty years. With pride he tells the story of how we made it to the seventeen-year marriage marker, longer than my first marriage. I've not stopped to count the number of years he was married to his previous eight wives, but I think I hold the record.

It's funny how personal historical memory and time have a way of softening and shading the past, blurring the hard lines.

When the words are on a page, they trigger remembrances and recollections, bringing back rough-edged memories, some with tremendous humor. There were horrific moments, simple misadventures, and missteps on a small and grand scale. There were times I wondered if we would live through events, and times I didn't even care.

We made it, a bit worse for the wear, but nevertheless we made it. What this means is that we are all alive—we're not all speaking to one another, but we're alive.

The names and some places have been changed to protect the not-so-innocent. It seemed to be a better compromise than footing the bill for three children in the witness protection program or lifelong therapy, though I support their request for anonymity and thank them for their inspiration. I am proud to have contributed a small fortune to nourish the 401(k) belonging to our numerous family therapists.

Meanwhile, this is every woman's story: love, loss, growth, failure, rise again, and repeat. The story of life. The story of my life.

In the Beginning

Seventy-five glorious degrees of Southern California sunshine on Doheny Drive, south of Sunset Boulevard, on a sunny Saturday June morning—how could I beat this? I was free of university life, a shade under twenty, and ready to begin my life. At that point, that meant finding an apartment close to my job and exploring the city that had been my new home for less than two weeks. Most people scour the closest grocery stores, dry cleaners, or specialty shops, but not me. I was on the lookout for the most incredible homes north of the Strip that I could ogle, dreaming about the inhabitants.

Having landed a job at a prestigious decorator's showroom on Robertson Boulevard, I was enchanted with design, fabrics, and the wealthy who could afford to hire designers to create their own personal ambiance. I had been a textile major in school and thought I had a flair for design, but the job, for which I had no formal training, was acquired due to the insistence of a friend of my mother's. The original insistence had been my own mother's, beseeching her oldest friend to help her only offspring. It would just be for a while, and I would come back to my senses. Mother saw me as mercurial, flighty, and one not to think things through to a logical conclusion. She likened the impulsive decision to leave conservative university life in the center of Texas and move to the unknown and certainly fearful City of the Angels, as a phase. She likened this phase to my high school boredom phase or the not-forgotten phase of wanting to be a boy when I was six. Phases were a sense of order and comfort for her, and she believed my phases were a necessary path toward my correct and final decision, which would open the door to true contentment. She didn't live to see me find the key to that door. Over the years when I expressed happiness in my work or my life, it was met with comments about working too hard, not having the right outward signs of success, or having dismal expectations about life's potential outcome. It has taken most of my life to understand her life's disappointments and her attempt to correct her mistakes through my life.

My family and I had settled in the Rio Grande Valley of the Lone Star State just as I was entering middle school, and I knew, once again, that I had been misplaced. Rural South Texas didn't hold much charm. By the time I turned fifteen, I'd figured my way out of high school in three years instead of four. If I could do it in high school, why not at university? Accomplishing high school in three years was a cakewalk, but college was different. I burned out and couldn't finish. I had taken on too much, but this was at odds with what my mother wanted for me: to finish school and settle down with a fine young man with an impeccable family tree, have children, and be happy. Since she had squashed my lifelong passion and study of dance and theatre with demands of a University education as opposed to my teachers and mentors belief I should move to New York or Las Vegas for a professional career, the thought she could continue to control my future was an inescapable normality. Never mind I had spent my entire young life on the stage, that potential career was not an option and was chalked up to an extra-curricular activity not worthy of pursuing after high school. The dance classes I taught in a pre-school and small dance studio during University days, was merely a way to make spending money and not considered an option for future employment.

I'm quite sure the conversation with her friend had been couched in her heady unreality that she saw as my not-too-distant future; settling down to a proper life; her vision of a proper life. So, with a promise to Mother that I wouldn't be on her friend's doorstep for long and that this would be a good learning experience, I moved into Park La Brea, a legendary edifice near the La Brea Tar Pits, catering to the senior crowd and thousands more. It is a sprawling apartment community with 4,255 units in the Miracle Mile District of Los Angeles, the largest housing development in the United States west of the Mississippi River. I was totally overwhelmed.

I learned that the elegant showroom of my employment represented the interior design world's most prestigious sources for exclusive fabrics, wallpapers, trimmings, furniture, and carpet, with a distinct and haughty point of view. It was exquisite. I had about as much business being in that upscale space, attempting to sell expensive fabric and antiques, as a mutt at Westminster. I was just nineteen, and my filters were skewed with a confidently attractive exterior and a soon-to-be-twenty air of assertiveness. I could hold my own, and I fearlessly met any potential transgressors. After all, I was from Texas, the land of women who can smell bullshit a mile away and sling it that far in a proper hat and white gloves. The Texan attitude considered the West Coast residents to be too liberal, too uptight, and—worse than anything—clueless about good barbeque. In the opinion of my Lone Star friends and acquaintances, I had moved to Mars.

With my limited classroom experience and knowledge of warp and woof as it applied to the rag trade, I openly learned how the real world worked as opposed to the textbook examples. I didn't reflect upon what I had left behind or the short timeframe in which I'd created a new reality. I didn't think about not having a long-term plan because I knew my mother would be there should I need her, or even should I fail. In her world, parental responsibility for offspring did not end until a wedding band was in place. I assumed this was normal and accepted her help as such.

I arrived in Los Angeles with a mattress tied to the roof of my car and the allowance my parents gave me for food and shelter, with no parameters as to when I would have to start supporting myself. With little knowledge of my future employment, I moved into the retirement community with the wonderful friend of my mother's who had twisted the arm of her gay brother for my job—to give the kid a break.

Lord only knows what that man thought when I showed up for work in a crisp, Kelly green and white minidress, white platform shoes, long platinum hair, and false eyelashes. In my defense, it was 1972, platform shoes were back in style, and it was after Memorial Day and before Labor Day, so the white shoes were appropriate according to my very Southern mother.

I didn't consider myself an enigma, I was simply me: friendly, intelligent, gracious, and ready to learn. Gracious goes with a Southern upbringing like a good country ham, grits, and biscuit breakfast—the art of charm, regardless of reality. Manners, alongside the love of football and barbeque, are ingrained survival assets. I never worried about being liked or fitting in. I just expected everything to work out. To their credit, the man and his professional colleagues welcomed their new charge, and I became the project of three terrific and diverse mentors.

I was much loved and at home in the new environment created by my three gay bosses, two men and a woman whose combined knowledge of design and sales equaled, at the very least, the mileage I had driven from Austin to Los Angeles. My knowledge was measured in inches, and my learning curve began at the foot of Mt. Everest.

They were so kind, taking me under their care, steering me to the correct wing of fabrics when the dreaded Palm Springs icon, Arthur Elrod, a regular customer, descended with his coterie of young, beautiful, perfectly tanned sycophants. Elrod, a regular customer with monied and discerning clientele, had a penchant for expensive fabrics, furniture, and *Architectural Digest* covers stories. I wasn't exactly thrown to the wolves, yet I had to prove my knowledge and show a legitimate reason for taking up space. Who better to test my acumen than a legend? He requested a Napoleonic Bee upholstery fabric. I either didn't know or didn't remember from textile history that this design had been chosen by Napoleon to link his reign to the origins of the French kings and the Roman Empire. Historians have called Napoleon charismatic, ambitious, driven, controlling, and psychopathological—and the honeybee, a symbol of resurrection, served his majesty's desire for immortality.

I remembered one and only one honeybee on an expensive

gold and white threaded sample. By sheer luck, it suited his taste. He bought massive amounts of yardage at hundreds of dollars a yard, and I was a heroine. I knew that experience was the cross between a fluke and a nudge in the right direction by my three guardians. This decorator was a design superstar, and I a lowly paid intern. My success on decorator's row was sealed, briefly.

During those glorious pre-smog LA days, I trotted around Beverly Hills soaking up the atmosphere created for the other half. It was a warm summer day when I was walking in a pedestrian zone and a shiny new gold (of course) Rolls Royce stopped. A handsome man smiled at me from behind the wheel and asked if I needed a ride. Well, Miss Texas had never seen a Rolls outside of a magazine, and he looked nice, so inside I popped! We motored a bit, and he mentioned he was an attorney. By the way, was I an actress? Had I been in possession of warning bells, this would have been a klaxon followed by Morse code SOS, but I was South Texas raised on "yes, ma'am," and "yes, sir" (not "no, sir") especially when speaking to apparently influential sirs.

After being escorted to the top floor of a random high-rise near Doheny and Sunset and by the grace of the Universe not maimed or murdered, I was offered a part in a film. This offer was contingent upon the no-clothing clause with auditions beginning immediately in his office. I demurred, yet over the course of the next few days I was pursued by the attorney, ostensibly for his client, with the promise of my choice of Mercedes, an apartment in a Sunset Strip condominium, and money (and quite a bit of it), as well as a legal document stating that I would be present and accounted for, twenty-four-seven, to the client. Well, the attorney seemed genuine and was nice enough, yet the offer seemed a bit stifling for my Aquarian wanderlust. I passed on signing the paperwork. Ah, I could have been Linda Lovelace—terrifying to think about in retrospect. The bottom line was that my Catholic upbringing couldn't see how I could go to confession with all that on my dance card.

~~~

I didn't have too many to tell about my escapades, though my bosses enjoyed my stories and were proud of my upstanding choices.

They couldn't protect me from the bald one—let's call him John—who appeared late one Friday afternoon shopping for fabric. John was an interior designer in the film business and department chair of a major production company's design team. He was searching for décor for a movie set currently being filmed at Paramount Pictures. Charismatic was the word. Intense was the vibration. I was drawn in like a minnow to the whale. Never mind that John was old enough to be my father and previously married four times—I bit, hook, line, and sinker. Our first date was at a marvelous 1970s landmark in the Wilshire District of Los Angeles, Tail of the Cock restaurant. I learned that John was the father of three, ages seventeen, ten, and nine—and unhappily married. I believed everything on face value, not questioning his story though I was conflicted. I resisted the sane urge to leave and never look back. I didn't hear the future, simply choosing what I felt at the time over common sense.

In less than six weeks, the doorbell rang in my newly rented and sparsely furnished Hollywood apartment. There stood John, the man to whom I would be wed within two years and share the next seventeen years of my young life. He proclaimed with cocksure bluster that I was the perfect reason he had freshly left his wife. I had thirty minutes to grab a weekend suitcase and be out the door to a love nest resort north of Los Angeles. My first reaction was to ask myself what the hell I had gotten myself into. The second reaction was to throw caution to the wind. What the hell, I'd better pack a bag.

My one-bedroom apartment with gold shag carpeting in the heart of Hollywood was a dive, but it was the first apartment where I'd lived alone, and I loved it. I lived alone for exactly thirty-three days before John moved in and immediately became terrifically unhappy. John, edging close to fifty years old, had come from a Malibu beach house with a pool and a view to the heart of Hollywood Homeless Adjacent, only two blocks north. There was Beverly Hills Adjacent, and then there was Hollywood Homeless Adjacent. I couldn't afford the former. He couldn't handle the latter and quickly bought a Hollywood Hills fixer-upper, an English Tudor inspired home of silent movie actor Lucien Littlefield. The house on Canyon Cove was my first home since leaving my childhood town in Michigan and moving year after year.

When he left his wife, he also briefly left their two children, who were to follow into their father's new life.

Within a matter of weeks, John and I were living together and surrounded by the mass confusion of a total remodel. The man moved quickly. I was holding on for dear life, loving every minute of the May/post-December relationship. He'd tell the story of how we met many times over the next seventeen years and never failed to mention it was unusual for him to shop at the design showroom where I had been working. He had exhausted his normal resource venues and decided, late on a Friday afternoon, to give the place a try. There was nothing to lose; he was out of ideas and maybe something would show itself. Fate?

When, six weeks after that fateful Friday afternoon meeting at the design room, I told my mother I had met someone, she was at first elated. When I mentioned he was thirty years my senior, the ensuing silence spoke volumes. She invented the mic drop with that phone call. My controlling Catholic mother must have been going through rosaries like a cloistered nun. Later I learned that my father simply said, "If we say anything, she'll do the opposite, so better stay quiet." He was a man of few words, incredible insight, and unending patience. After all, he had lived with my mother for thirty years. This alone would have given him entrance to heaven.

I dodged that bullet of parental scorn, perhaps, but ended up at the end of another smoking gun—the unwanted scorn from my mother about being in a relationship with someone so many years my senior and living in Catholic-created sin, meaning no marriage paperwork. She would later point out that he was much closer to her age than mine, a veiled comment regarding the lack of longevity in my nonunion. Hell would be my reward if we didn't legalize the relationship, as would economic disaster.

Two years later, in 1974, in order to quiet the endless nagging, we staged a mock wedding event reported to be in the historic Santa Barbara Mission. We had photos taken in front of John's parents' Spanish duplex, which bore a striking resemblance to the Mission exterior, in the Wilshire District of Los Angeles. The charade continued with an elaborate celebration after the contrived wedding—complete with engraved invitations asking for no gifts please, as "the pleasure of your company is your gift to us"—catered luncheon, a gorgeous wedding cake, and a three-week honeymoon to Europe.

In June 1976, two years from the manufactured matrimony, a ceremony at Wee Kirk O' the Heather Wedding Chapel in Las

Vegas with Reverend Whitehead officiating made it legal without any flourish. The lengths I went to continue my non-conformist destiny!

Each year for five years John bought a new Los Angeles home to move into and renovate, each one made more incredible than the last due to his design flair and ability to turn a fixer-upper into a showplace. I learned volumes from my first mentor/husband. I relished his attention, his notoriety, his innate talents, and his care for my training. Being only recently past my chronological childhood, I grew under his tutelage and experience. In a George Bernard Shaw, *Pygmalion/My Fair Lady* story line, I was living with an accomplished husband/adult who'd had four previous marriages as well as expertise in a host of extended hobbies. I learned a lot by listening and observing.

John announced I needed proper training and, true to his nature of expecting the best, he sent me to the best schools. The first was a cooking school. It wasn't a stove and refrigerator in a small corner of a shop selling kitchen gadgets, it was a proper school, one run by a Cordon Bleu graduate. The months of learning how to sharpen a knife, bone a chicken, and make chicken Kiev in the original obscenely time-consuming and butter-laden manner would stay with me for the rest of my years. I adored cooking school, which then extended to a flower arranging school, cake decorating school, a pastry course, and four years later, real estate school. God, I hated real estate. The man who ran the school on Hollywood Boulevard was a predator. He was married to a well-known actress at the time, yet he had an eye for most anything in a skirt, or shorts, or a pair of tight pants. In no time, I was studying for my license under his personal tutelage. I was devoted to John and resisted this other man's advances, again and again. I wish I had not been frozen, unable to make a decision on how to handle an impropriety. The overwhelming feeling of being at fault for something that wasn't my doing and not seeing that I had options other than silence was difficult to process at the time. It was easier to pretend the advances didn't happen.

Real estate school was the perfect partner for John's talent for a remodel. As we worked our way through the difficulty of living in each remodel, John and I made memories surrounding the mutual desire to get ahead and ultimately move from the population explosion in Los Angeles. There was great challenge in turning out a French menu on a two-burner hotplate in a garage while the kitchen upstairs was gutted to the studs. I was young enough to believe this inconvenience to be fun.

Over the course of the years, this cottage industry allowed us to move from wild Southern California to parts more civilized—or at least the less inhabited coastal region south of San Francisco. We worked side by side to grow our small real estate empire, raised his daughter from age ten to high school graduation, traveled on location films, buried his mother, and took in his father.

Had my John been half as wonderful as his father, we would surely never have gotten a divorce.

His dad, J. R., would end up living with us for ten years—and not in a guest house but in the next bedroom. You couldn't have asked for a better long-term houseguest. He paid a share of his upkeep, went to the grocery store, had his own life with friends, read to the children, loved the dogs and cleaned up after them, fed the cat, and, above all, adored me. He taught me unconditional love repeatedly. He called me "baby doll" and was only cross with me once that I remember.

Cross is a word we don't hear much anymore, but it fit his personality. In 1982, after ten years of marriage, I was quite the hostess. I was having a dinner party and testing J. R.'s unending patience. I sent him to the grocery store at least five times to obtain forgotten items. The final trip was accomplished after his audible sigh and a sincere promise of the final trip. The setup included: a table for ten in the proper dining room, help in the kitchen, matching silver and china polished to a gleam, host and hostess dressed for dinner as were the guests, soft music in the background, martinis before dinner, and then the dinner. Oh my. At least four, perhaps five courses were prepared by me, the hostess, with much *oohing* and *ahhhing* as each dish was presented to the guests.

The next day the entire event was entered into a small black book, courtesy of the Horchow Collection, the first luxury mail-order catalog sold to Neiman Marcus in 1988 and the requisite bastion of taste for any Southern woman of the 1970s and 1980s, as a souvenir of who sat where at the table, what was served, and tidbits of conversation. My mother's Southern inspiration and training on the importance of how to conduct a proper household stayed with me, even though the Southern mindset wasn't as celebrated in California.

When my father-in-law moved in, I was twenty-two, and John's children were ten, eleven, and eighteen. The eighteen-year-old soon enlisted in the armed services to escape, and we were left with the younger children. The bookstore shelves at that time were not lined with titles reflecting the best coping skills for a new stepparent, how to raise stepchildren from hell, how to relate to the ex, or anything remotely helpful to a new stepmother with children who should have been siblings instead of wards. I certainly made every mistake in the book.

As a young child, I dreamed of one day having a family. I would sit by the hour and rudimentarily draw houses for the anticipated and expected adoring husband and two children: one girl, Megan Elizabeth, and an unnamed boy. My dream space had a large playroom where both children would play peacefully, grow in love for each other, and give years of joy to their parents. They would attend the proper schools, have proper weddings, and live proper lives.

In the very beginning of our dating, I made it clear to John that I wanted children. John and I talked at length about how important a baby was to me. Even though he had three by two different previous wives, he was on board.

But it didn't come easily to me. Perhaps if we could have stopped the madness of raising two kids and moving yearly and just had some quiet time, things would have been different. Having been a performer, I attributed my lack of normal menstrual periods to my exercise/performance schedule. I was a healthy twenty-two-year-old. There was nothing wrong with me.

But, it turns out there was. I was diagnosed with cervical cancer a year into our marriage and was admitted to St. John's Hospital in Santa Monica, a bastion of excellence in clinical care. Founded in 1942 as a private Catholic hospital by the Catholic Sisters of Leavenworth, it was a benchmark in the world of medicine for compassionate care. Since I was in my daily Catholic mass phase, it was a perfect fit. In the mid-1970s, this type of diagnosis was not prevalent and required a two-night stay in the hospital for a cone biopsy. I was admitted to the cancer ward, sharing a room with a woman who was days away from dying, crying out day and night for more morphine to ease her pain and undergoing a torturous weighing process to ascertain how much weight she had lost daily.

I was in a living nightmare and couldn't make sense of why I was there in the hospital. After all, daily mass, Catholic hospital, prayers, and rosaries weren't making a difference. I felt abandoned. The hardest part was not being able to do anything to comfort the woman next to me. I ached to reach out and touch her, yet I was confined to my bed and she to hers. We could only talk through the stale green curtain that separated our humanity but not our compassion.

I was the lucky one. I got to go home with the cancer behind me.

We had not used any contraception, and, with no pregnancies, I consulted my gynecologist. The battery of tests and another hospitalization for me gave us a diagnosis: anovulation, or lack of egg production. This could be helped with a drug, Clomid, a baby-boosting fertility drug. There were strong warnings that there was a chance of multiple births and some uncomfortable side effects, yet I was invincible. This wouldn't take long to achieve: procure a proper basal thermometer, basal temperature graph, and attention to the timing of the drug-induced ovulation via the chart was all that was required.

After a few months, the reality set in. There was a twenty-four-hour time period of optimum fertility, and that was the once-a-month chance to conceive. I can tell you it certainly takes the romance out of the game.

Month after month this repeated. A year went by, and then another. In total it took from 1972, when we first met, until 1981 to have a child. Seven of those years I was on and off Clomid.

At one point, I simply gave up. I was tired of the tears, the frustration, the charts, and the infernal thermometer. I was tired of seeing children everywhere, even in my dreams. I was done, really done.

We left for a location feature movie shoot together, destined never to have a child. Where better to forget than the City by the Bay? The weather was glorious, and the company had leased a flat for our stay on Pacific Street with an incredible view of the water. I would either accompany John on location or shop the streets below our three-month home, have a coffee, browse the bookstores, and generally enjoy life.

Wine tasting in Napa with John and my parents, who were visiting from their home in Arizona, changed our lives. Two days after visiting Christian Brothers Winery, the famous Greystone Cellars, and fainting in the perfectly chilled tasting room, the doctor confirmed a baby had created that swoon. Nine months later I gave birth to my first son, Ashton, alone, having been driven to the hospital a short hour before delivery by J. R., my seventy-five-year-old father-in-law who had been pleading with me to get to the hospital for the four previous hours. My mind had left the building, and I didn't remember one thing about labor, breathing, contractions—zip, nada, nothing. Had it not been for that sweet elderly man, a child would have been born at home with grandpa in attendance.

My firstborn son's father, John, was on location and arrived early the next morning to kiss my head, look at his son, and declare he had to go back to work and that everything was going to be fine.

I should have known then there was something not quite right.

After a drama-filled three days at home, I hopped on a plane with my infant bound for Reno, where said film was being shot, and joined the baby's father in a hotel for the duration of the shoot. Ashton slept in the bottom drawer of the chest of drawers in the hotel room for two months.

Life on the road for three years at multiple movie locations deserves its own book. It was a time of great adventure, incredible travel, and an intact family—not typical, but at least intact. John's two older children were in boarding school near our Central Coast home and could come home on the weekends, if they chose, to visit with their grandfather. When we were home from a location, they would join us for family dinners, a movie—a normal family.

On the road was sometimes a reality sitcom with adventures of epic proportions. I blew out the electrical panel in an entire wing of the Great Smokies Hilton while cooking in the room for eight hungry film crew members—too many hot plates and woks going at the same time to accommodate a dinner party. From El Paso to Banff, and Los Angeles to Amityville, New York, the swathe of outages is legendary, and so are the stories. Life wasn't real. It was a movie set, and frankly, much preferable to reality. It's no wonder actors fall in love on the set and then divorce when the film ends and life gets real.

Preschool loomed for Ashton, and a decision was made for Mommy and child to stay at home while John continued to travel on location. The common thread of thought in schooling in the mid-1980s included the proper preschool as a precursor to the proper elementary education, which was followed by the proper high school and culminated in your choice of university for higher education and the world being placed at your child's feet. Cue hands brushing together, and all is done for the lifetime warranty. By choice, I was homebound and immersed myself in the day-to-day working of the school: volunteering for committees, baking cookies, running rummage sales, and weekly trips to swimming lessons, piano lessons, and gymnastics. Very typical and safe—I was safe and my child was safe.

Our second child, Scooter, was born in a Pitocin vengeance after another two years of fertility treatments. John was between films and ready to travel on the next at any moment, and the baby was term, so what the hell? My OB-GYN called it a social delivery. My decision to deliver on an appointed day was due to John's schedule. In my later years, I'd realize that "what the hell?" isn't always the best way to go.

Fricking Pitocin is what the hell—zero to 120 in one second. But I got what I wanted—again—Baby Daddy present; a nine-pound, two-ounce baby boy who rocketed out of my vagina and didn't pass go. Should have known then he was going to be a wild ride.

I gave my first two male children dolls for their first birthdays. The first one looked at it and gently put it down, never to pick it up again; the second one tried with all of his might to use it as a hammer to destroy anything in sight. He had great hand-to-eye coordination.

My go-to book was *Growing Up Free: Raising Your Child in the 80's,* by Letty Cottin Pogrebin. Children's first birthday presents were supposed to be symbols of unfettered child-rearing via updated social norms and no restrictions. On the occasion, I received indifference and tool-sharing. The '80s: a time of feminine shoulder pads the size of a defensive linebacker's, big teased hair, and loud makeup. What were we thinking? The 1980s were fraught with economic downturns and a second wave of the feminist revenge against the 1940s and *Leave It to Beaver*. My mother wasn't June Cleaver. She ran a successful business in Michigan. I remember a snowy weekday when the driver wouldn't deliver a load of unevenly tied two-by-fours up a snow-covered and daunting hill. My mother got in the truck, drove the damn thing up the hill, got out, and handed him the keys with a big smile. If she could do it all in the '50s, I could certainly do it all in the '80s.

Life raising two wasn't too bad with a revolving door of nannies to assist. They were mostly very young European girls, many from small Austrian villages on their first time away from home, some scared, and some homesick. Many were terrific.

John's work took him away for months at a time, and, when the middle child turned two, being apart began to take its toll. I was invited to a holiday dinner party and seated next to a handsome single man. The evening was filled with silent flirtations, unwavering eye contact, and a stolen good-night kiss. It was ego refreshing to be considered attractive, and yet my warning system was unusually engaged. I had learned a valuable lesson during the Rolls Royce and real estate school capers, and I figured honesty was the best policy in affairs of the heart. So with a deep breath, I made a midnight phone call and begged John to come home from location. I told him what had happened that night, that I hadn't wanted it to happen, and that I needed him. I believed if I were truthful, certainly I wouldn't be chastised or blamed. We could work this out. Couldn't we meet? Could I fly to him?

He simply said, "You are having an affair." The telephone clicked, and the discussion was over. I wasn't having an affair, and my need to be heard was rebuffed. I'd imagined my confession would be met with compassion, understanding, and a willingness to discuss options. Nothing was further from the truth.

If someone could figure out how to change hindsight into foresight, they would make a fortune and save the world at the same time. John's answer to my request was to revert to his wanton ways and become the roué he had been before we married. Seeing that he was on wife number five, there clearly wasn't a track record of fidelity. Soon there were many nights when the hotel room phone wasn't answered, and a flimsy excuse about work was offered one too many times. His stories and alibis didn't line up, and I awakened to the fact that, even though I was in the prime of my life, he either wasn't satisfied or he was filled with the need for a vengeful and spite-ridden episode. If I had even thought about being with someone else in a potential affair, he could do it better. He could have the affair. The last straw was when he came home from an East Coast film set and suggested I take up singing lessons. Singing lessons? Seriously? Then I found out he was sleeping with a lounge singer. I guess he wanted the crooning to continue when he came home.

It was clear to me that I had been honest with my feelings, and he had chosen to retaliate. I was done with the marriage, and no amount of counseling would change my mind. Moreover, I cannot sing.

I knew my simplistic views of marriage and child-rearing had taken a 180 while I wasn't looking, but wanting out and getting out are two very distinct issues. I had begun to teach a couple days a week to get out of the house and back to the world I loved. It certainly wasn't enough to live on if I chose to divorce. My mother kindly reminded me, on a regular basis, that I would be the first one in the history of her family to get a divorce. I bit my tongue. She and my dad certainly were not a match made in heaven. Would they have been better off had they chosen to separate? We would never know, but the glory and familial honor of the D-word would be mine and mine alone.

The profound surprise was the third pregnancy—with no fertility drugs and completely unplanned, and the result of a weekend home from his East Coast location. At thirty-two, I had a six-year-old and a two-year-old at home, and I had been working up the strength to ask for a divorce after that location shoot was finished.

I was *what*?

I was trapped, and off he went again to god knows where on god knows what movie and to god knows what new conquest. My safe paradise had become a hellhole of depression where I allowed the Kingdom of Rage, Anger, and Fear to reign for a few days before picking myself up, buying some new maternity wear, and putting on a smiling face. When you have no choice, you get dressed, put on your makeup, and fake it. Another key to Southern charm.

A baby girl with piercing blue eyes arrived without much fuss in the cold hours of a December morning. I had been directing a play that closed its run the night before, and, with the holidays approaching, the look of the family was perfect. Christmas tree decorated, check. Presents wrapped, check. Lots of presents wrapped, check. Beautiful and clean children dressed for church, check. Miserable parents, check. The divorce proceedings would come one year later.

I had to hatch a plan to secure my future, as I knew the baby's daddy would not be part of said future. The only thing I knew how to do was teach. The last of the money my parents had scrimped and saved for my inheritance became a down payment on a building in the heart of downtown. That was the last time my husband and I closed a real estate deal together. It would become an icon of the village in the arts education of young people thirty years later. At the time, I had no earthly idea what the hell I was doing. Had I waited to know what I was doing; I would still be stuck. I put one foot in front of the other every day for the next thirty years because I had no choice. I knew the drill: get dressed, put on your makeup, smile.

Life delivers choices, though not always as clear as A + B = C. My highly intuitive stubborn streak and I made choices and worked with the consequences. At the time, I saw no options. I wanted out then and there. Take what you want and leave what you will; just leave me alone. This wouldn't my advice today to those embarking on the rocky road of single parenthood. I would have insisted on half of everything—plus alimony and child support. I opted out of everything except child support. I didn't need anyone and could do this all on my own, or at least that was my stubborn, bull-headed, and minefield-laden reasoning. My world was reduced to a paltry $300 per month child support, no alimony after seventeen years of marriage, and debt beyond my dreams.

Imagine, he took me at my word when I said, "Take everything, I just want out"—and the moving van took every stick of antique furniture we had collected over those long years of marriage. He was mad, and he took that anger to his grave. That didn't stop him from marrying twice after our divorce, once to a young woman who checked his groceries at an upscale grocery store in Malibu, and then to his first wife, Adele, for the second time. His first wife took him back. Hard to believe, but true.

Altogether he had eight marriages and six children. His dream had always been to have all his children at the same dinner table, amiably chatting about how terrific a father he had been. Cue Robert Goulet singing, "The Impossible Dream."

When he later died at age seventy-nine, I would track down the probate attorney, as our youngest was under eighteen. I wanted to know if there were any provisions in the will for her. I explained who I was and the fact we had been married for seventeen years and had three children together. The attorney's comment was, "I've never heard of you or the three children." It was the ultimate act of controlling—from the grave. I had documentation, birth certificates, and deeds of trust, yet when I considered contesting, the cold reality of attorney fees and the legal battle with John's three children by previous marriages wasn't worth it. The Wonder Woman in me knew I could do it, whatever "it" was, without anyone. I believed the lie that women can do it all and have it all. What a fool!

I currently counsel soon-to-be-divorced women seeking my advice: Don't be fooled by your heart. Use your head and fight for what is fair for you and your children. I don't believe all men are bad and all women are financially abused in divorce, yet if you don't stand up and fight for what is fair, there is only one person to blame. There are so many ways to go into a union with peace of mind; a prenuptial agreement is a great example and one I wish I'd had. This document can and should be written to protect both sides in case of a divorce. It puts all the assets and debts on the table before the union, ultimately starting with a clean slate. It can be a voice of reason in a sea of emotion should there be a contentious future. The peace of mind in marrying for love and not money is the best defense for a prenuptial agreement.

The years immediately following two years of divorce court appearances by our respective attorneys only served the purpose of creating income for the two attorneys. By this time, I had moved out of the fairytale family home and was living in eight hundred square feet with the three kids and driving the car of my previous life's dream, a 1985 Corvette convertible (not quite the appropriate car for a single mother with three young children). He got the Lincoln Town Car, a condo in Solvang—the City of Eternal Christmas—and the trappings that had been our life together. The karma was to know he was living in a town with "Shop, Mingle, and Jingle" as their Christmas marketing slogan.

I was now a single mother raising three children and a full-time fledgling entrepreneur in a struggling business. I had to give up the concept of being the perfect mother. The dream of raising responsible, incredible children who would impact the world in a positive manner and, more importantly, not have temper tantrums on the floor at the local bank was snuffed. Yet, responsibly (and according to the norm of the '80s, remember), I could have it all and do it all. Gloria Steinem and Betty Friedan, leading figures in the women's movement, had given me permission to be indefatigable. I was young, and I believed. The reality was harsh.

The family home had been leased, and I was determined to save the property for the future of my children. I envisioned moving back one day and set about making up the difference between rent and mortgage by selling a piece of jewelry each month at the reputable local hock shop. Retrospectively, I am sure they took some pity on my monthly visits and soon-to-be-paltry offerings, yet I was able to forestall the selling of that three-thousand-square-foot beauty for over a year. Eventually, though, I ran out of things to sell.

Two years after the sale of the family home, I was confronted with the fact that if I didn't purchase a home in sixty days, I would owe the IRS $30,000 in capital gains tax. I didn't have $30,000 or any way to come up with it in sixty days, so I contacted Joanne, a real estate agent, and told my story.

Her friend, a mortgage broker name Heidi, my future guardian angel—said quite bluntly, "We're going to look at the good, the bad, and the ugly in the debt column. Bring every bit of paperwork you have and meet me in my office tomorrow morning at nine." Joanne went to work on what rubble that meeting would purchase. I was there, and it was ugly, yet there was a light of hope and a ray of sunshine amidst the chaos.

Joanne, the real estate angel, chauffeured me to three very different living experiences. Not being one to waste time, she told me point blank that the three choices were all I had, and I needed to make up my mind at the end of this tour.

The three choices were: 1) close to a high school with lots of yard and a roof that needed repair; 2) in a flood plain; and 3) a condominium. It was an easy choice. I knew my children would never lift a hand to mow the yard, so the first was out. House 2 in the flood plain was not an option. I didn't relish the idea of a fleet of boats attempting to rescue four roof-floating inhabitants of said property in the middle of a hurricane. By default, and with no other choice (a theme, wouldn't you say?), the condo on the meadow became home for our motley crew. It took every penny to get us in the door, which left nothing for new paint or carpet. Green shag carpet and harvest gold appliances looked heaven-sent to me after four years of dwelling in compartmentalized spaces on the same property as my work. I owned a home and had full custody of Ashton, fifteen, Scooter, eleven, and Cinnamon, nine. Finally, everything was going to work out!

Workdays were longer and harder, and many weeks were seven-day, sixteen-to-eighteen-hour marathons. In the years to come, I'd look back and wonder how I did it. I don't think I thought; I just did because there was no choice. Many realities were boldfaced. No furniture for the living room and bedrooms, three children in three different schools, and no father figure. He had moved south, and, except for an occasional visit, the kids rarely saw him.

The two older children would suffer then, and later, more quietly, our daughter. The middle one was loud, wild, and medicated, the perfect storm from hell waiting to assert its fury on the unsuspecting. There had been talk from his teachers about learning differences since he'd entered first grade, yet I had no idea what was to materialize in the not-so-distant future. Having been medicated for six years on Adderall and Ritalin specifically, he was not only the epitome of the middle child, he had the types of behavior that, in the late 1980s and early 1990s, were just beginning to be addressed by schools and clinicians.

As a single mother, I continued to pretend I could take anger issues, medication ups and downs, and serious depression in stride.

This created the imminent need for innovation and required expectation and follow-through.

It was a hard reality that I would not be able to stay awake to welcome my precious brood home from a school dance, to hear about their evening with a girlfriend, to share in the drama of young couples on a date, or to give my incredibly sage advice to mend a broken heart, all over homemade hot chocolate and perfect gingersnap cookies. They didn't give a damn about my sage advice and were probably happy they weren't facing me at the door with their flimsy excuse for being drunk, stoned, or late for curfew.

From an early age, I believed I was destined to be one of those perfect mothers. I know some of them—the women with unsmudged manicures and matching pedicure polish, coordinated outfits, shoes, and handbags. They never had a drop of breast milk leakage, a dry vagina, or hangnails. Their children graduated cum laude from Princeton, having had a newspaper route that paid the tuition and a second high school job as the manager of a store at the mall paying for room and board. These mothers were highly intellectual professionals with careers that spanned the globe, adoring husbands in three-piece suits, and two late-model cars. They were home every evening at five for one cocktail while awaiting a gourmet dinner.

I can assure you; I was not one of these.

The idea of the notes, which have become *Notes after Midnight,* was born out of necessity. I had to trust my children because I needed one thing: sleep. I tactfully explained to my three kids that if I saw their note under the door by two in the morning, I would refrain from calling the local hospitals and police station to find out if they were dead. How embarrassing would it be for the entire cast of three characters, should they be tucked in bed upstairs and dreaming peacefully having arrived home well before curfew, to find the sheriff's department at the front door? Since they knew I was a worrying sort, this was the most efficient way for me to not have a complete breakdown in the middle of the night and not incur the title "nut case" from the local authorities.

There was no particular plan for these notes. They were hatched in a family meeting, one of those moments when everyone sits together in one room and attempts to agree—though loud sighs and eye-rolling are more prevalent than actual solutions. The meetings were concrete and short, with brief bullet points regarding appropriate behavior designed to keep me appeased, and each child accepted the note delivery challenge. I didn't think that one day this would become a project resulting in a book about my life raising teenagers. I am not a hoarder, but I would end up keeping most of my children's things. Don't those perfect mothers do the same? All of their children's memorabilia are in color-coded scrapbooks with nonsmudge calligraphy headings from first breath to marriage. But I am not one of those.

Years after they all left home, I would run into the folder with over two hundred notes.

I sorted them out, child by child, fascinated by pecking order and how each of the sets of notes said something so unique about each child: Ashton, the eldest, eager to please, reliable and ambitious, is a storyteller. Scooter, the quintessential middle child, is a peacemaker and an independent entrepreneur. Cinnamon, the baby, is narcissistic, artistic, self-indulgent, and spoiled.

In all families, there are trials, tribulations, exaltation, exhaustion, and days of ecstatic belief that it is all going to be OK. Sometimes it isn't all OK. Sometimes it doesn't work out, yet the ubiquity of human conflict leads us to one word: hope.

Ashton

Ashton: April 28, 1981

Eyes: Brown

Hair: Brown

- Intellectual firstborn, cautious, independent thinker, assertive, motivated, and mature
- Stubborn, and happy to tell you he rules the realm.

"Raising children is an uncertain thing. Success is reached only after a life of battle and worry."
—Democritus

Dear All—
We have a fugitive.
He's furry.
Last seen cavorting with butterflies
Please catch him, as he was
acting juvenile and aloof in my
presence, despite offers of
food and crunchies

The fugitive was Loki, the free cat, named after the Norse god of mischief. He was a trickster who conned his way into our hearts. His attachment to Ashton grew particularly strong over the years. The pet adoption event is pivotal, as it would be the first of many attempts for Reg, the man who would become the stepparent, to make points. Reg was the man I had chosen to inherit the title of father to my children after their biological father abdicated most of his responsibilities, including but not limited to financial, emotional, physical, and educational. There were men who wanted to date, live in, and take me on vacation, but few who chose to accept this difficult task of shared parenting, the very thing I was in search of. Reg embraced the challenge, gave his love and care to my children unconditionally, and called them his. It took me a year and half to say yes to the marriage proposal, and during that time he continued to prove himself. He was not without fault, which Ashton pointed out immediately upon recognition of a lasting relationship as a mark of Reg's inferiority, yet to me it was not a deterrent. Each child had their own take on the relationship.

Ashton, sixteen, was not going to have much to do with this interloper; Scooter was twelve and a self-absorbed Petri dish of problems; and Cinnamon was eight and simply wanted to be loved and have a real daddy who showed up to sporting events. Her testing the limits with the kitten became the stuff of family legend.

The saga began on the playing field on a warm October afternoon. Cinnamon, a soccer jock at eight years old, was at Saturday game day. Mother (me) was working as usual, so Reg was in the role of dutiful dad that day, taking Rice Krispies bars and Capri Suns to the team. A friend's cat had had kittens, and this friend shamelessly brought them to a soccer field filled with captive young children to make sure she found a good home for each of them in less than an hour. "May I *pleeeeeeese* have a kitty?" Cinnamon begged. "I've never wanted or asked for anything before and I never will again, if I can just have this kitten."

Now, where on earth do they get that line? "Never asked before and will never ask again." They must think we are clueless. Reg must have been daft to fall hook, line, and catnip for that one.

I arrived home, late as usual, to find a new member of the already quite dysfunctional splinter group designated as my family. Everyone was happy as a lark, except for me, since I knew I'd be the one whose responsibility the fur ball would be for the rest of its life.

High drama arose one evening about a year later when said feline did not return home for dinner or for the night. Guess who marched around the outside of the house shaking a bag of crunchies at three in the morning? I can assure you it was no one under sixteen, nor was it the man of the house. Still, no cat.

Lunchtime the next day produced a bloodied boy kitty and two hysterical human parents dashing to the vet and managing to cancel a fundraising lunch at the same time. The famous words rolled easily off my tongue, "It doesn't matter how much it costs, save his life." Now there's another line that hasn't been taught; it just blurts without forethought or reason. Perhaps it stems from ancient chivalry, the need to please, or a momentary aneurism. Whatever the reason, *they*, whoever they are, take you at your word.

The cat had lost one eye to a car or a raccoon, we never knew for sure. I do know it was only one of three times when I ever saw my firstborn cry: seeing his beloved cat on the brink of death, when his first love was unrequited, and when the aforementioned feline died. The cat, perhaps losing two of its nine lives, lived to be a sprightly seventeen years old. On brief moments of escape from its prison/home, it could down a hummingbird like an incoming ballistic missile.

Have this funny feeling
like I'm supposed to do
something tomorrow, I
can't remember what . . .
Could you tell me in
the morning?
Sleep Well,
Ashton

Could I tell him what he needed to do in the morning? Wow, the trust factor in that loaded question is awesome! I can't remember what I needed to tell him, but I later learned that I apparently didn't tell any of them what they needed to hear: life lessons. By the time they were ready to listen, it was a game of survival, and most days it wasn't pretty. I worked seven days a week building the business—a performing arts conservatory featuring fine arts training—and hoped for the best at home. By the best, I meant the four walls would be upright and in their original position when I walked in twelve or fourteen hours after I'd left. Not being the perfect mother was frustrating and depressing. I was sure others' homes were spotless. I was sure the children's clothes in those homes were color-coded, folded with a knife edge, and safely tucked into fabric-lined drawers that were color coordinated to the wallpaper in their bedroom.

My closet didn't hold the right outfit for every occasion, much less the next day. I didn't get what I wanted, yet, as I look back, I got what I needed—barely. When I asked one of my three-year-old students what they wanted to be when they grew up, I got a solid no-nonsense answer: "A princess." This kid at three was a hell of a lot smarter than I was at thirty-five. So, maybe the kids got lessons in life, just different from other children. They could find enough quarters in the sofa for a couple gallons of gas to get them to school, and they learned to be strong in the face of adversity. Maybe that is the best lesson after all.

Its 4:30 a.m. and I'm going to hate
life tomorrow
See you at 9:15
Sleep Well,
Ashton

I had wanted children for as long as I could remember. I had the names picked out early on, as well as the dream wedding, dream house, and dream life. I don't remember picking the dream father. I guess I passed over on that dream. But kids were always in the picture.

The theory of pecking order wasn't one that I studied until I had multiple children. There is something to be said for the significance of birth order. This theory was first championed by Austrian physician Alfred Adler in the 1920s, but despite his wealth of work, many of his findings have since been dismissed due to a lack of scientific reasoning.

According to Adler, firstborns were likely to enjoy higher achievements, middle children a higher level of sociability, the youngest to be the most rebellious, and only children he believed to be successful yet selfish.

My eldest exhibited (and stills does) the four major characteristic of the firstborn: confident, hardworking, ambitious, and competitive. Raising the first one is a series of guessing games if you don't have a role model to learn from. The typical role model is your own mother or the mother of the father of the child. My mother didn't breastfeed, didn't understand that newborns' feeding routines are not subject to strict schedules, and didn't carry me around in a sling across her chest. She also must have had me baptized while exiting the birth canal, as she informed me, three days after Ashton was born, that if I didn't get the baby baptized ASAP, he wouldn't go to heaven. I was holding him too much, she said. Let him cry it out, she said. And I was obviously starving the child by breastfeeding because he always wanted to nurse. That's when I told her to go home. Home was ten hours and sixteen minutes away, so it was a rather traumatic goodbye.

Ashton's father left a few hours after his birth for a location film, and I was left alone with nursing issues, no one to talk to, and little direction. Doulas didn't exist in 1981, and I was the poster child for not knowing what to do with an infant. So, I did what every other woman in my hormonal hell would have done: I got on a plane with my five-day-old baby to meet my husband in Reno, Nevada, on the film shoot. "Here I am," I told him. "You've got to help me fix this mess." Of course, I had taken the classes, but in the '80s the classes were about the birth with not too much about the afterward part. I hadn't done a lot of babysitting in my life, so guessing was the next best option. Good thing I was pretty good at multiple-choice.

⌒‿⌒

11:48
Good Evening
Dinner and slideshow with Roberta
All is well . . . no witticisms tonight (sorry)
Please wake me for work
tomorrow
Sleep Well
Ashton

My firstborn, a budding intellectual, was a warm and loving little boy who became cold and guarded with his feelings, a definite behavioral change beginning at twelve years old that coincided with the beginning of the middle school experience. Until the curtains drew closed on his feelings—they would stay that way far into his twenties—I'd somehow deluded myself into believing that my presence would be enough to avoid divorce damage. He'd been a typical small boy, all noise and motion. He'd slept in a hotel chest of drawers for three years while I followed his father from job to job. Then preschool loomed. If you didn't get your child into the right preschool, you were destined to be rearing a future homeless person. We want them to live, thrive, and persevere—not too much to ask. The perfect mothers wanted to protect their kids from a world that would swallow them whole if we took our eyes off them for even a moment. I was one of those, for a few years. I remember a time when I believed the story I had made up about myself more than I should have. The story was about my self-importance since, after all, my husband had an executive position. I was a trophy wife before the term was coined. During many of those years, I adopted an air of youthful arrogance and self-imposed distinction. This truth does not make me proud.

Still, the perks of an LA film-based career were pretty terrific—until the divorce, that is. Then I became one of the others: the women pitied for being alone and raising children. The women who *had* to work to make ends meet, who no longer got invited to dinner, and whose friends took sides and ultimately disappeared altogether.

The lesson for them and for the others is simple: nothing turns out the way you plan. And if you say it has, you're lying.

Their father left when Ashton was eight, his siblings four and two. The fallout from our decision to separate, which I participated in to the fullest, would have long-term ramifications. In 2003, when their father was dying, twenty-two-year-old Ashton said, "Just let me know when he dies."

When his inevitable death occurred—I'm ashamed to admit it was not soon enough for me—I learned quickly there were no provisions in his will or potential inheritance for the children born from our seventeen-year union. Upon my telephone inquiry, the attorney casually mentioned the deceased had never mentioned our children, our marriage, or those seventeen years together.

People can really hold on to hard feelings. They say (who-ever *they* are) that moral contempt or hate is the same as love. The results were nowhere close to the same, and the children got to deal with that for the rest of their lives.

I will never understand the complete impact of abandon-ment on the first child. I am keenly aware of the effect on the middle and youngest. It was apparent that the middle school experience coupled with John's abandonment of his children created an atmosphere conducive to failure for an otherwise well-adjusted and high-functioning fifth-grader. When he entered middle school, it was as if another child took possession of my sweet son: homework not finished, reports not turned in, and a general procrastination not evident in the lower grades.

> *Hi,*
> *Very sorry about the wine deal today. The donations*
> *lady said that she didn't know about the wine, so I*
> *assumed I heard wrong on the phone—*
> *I hope Scooter got picked up OK. Tell me if there is*
> *anything I can*
> *do to make it up to you.*
> *Ashton*

The first child to get the much-anticipated driver's license arrives with much parental fear and trepidation. I attempted to allay any fears with my sincere belief that Ashton was capable, cau-tious, sensible, rational, and comparatively reasonable. That was my conscious mind doing the talking. My subconscious mind struggled to breathe regularly and control a racing heartbeat after eleven o'clock on a Saturday night while he was out with friends. My emotional mind repeated the local hospital emergency room number like a mantra and resisted the urge to call the sheriff's department to inquire about any recently reported automobile accidents. Daytime driving, for some reason, was not as terrifying for me, as it consisted of the list of errands it was necessary to accomplish before his evening outings could commence. He always had a list, and that list was varied. The wine deal mentioned in the note above connected a story from his youth, specifically in the third grade, to an errand necessary to complete a circle in an upcoming fundraising event.

Third grade is a magical year for children. Their reading skills are strong, and they're learning to see books as a source of information. During that year, reading can become a major interest because of the child's longer attention span. In Ashton's class, the kids, learning through interactive experiences, introduced a biography of their choice by transforming themselves into their notable and historic character.

Biography day was open to the parents and hosted by the most incredible and best-loved teacher in Ashton's private school. She was a legend, and students and parents alike awaited this event with great expectation. Not only would you be able to read your book report to the entire class, you would arrive dressed as the character. Our single-parent home was filled with dance and music, specifically ballet and classical leanings that framed the performing arts academy I had founded in 1989. True to his home life upbringing, his book report was about Mikhail Baryshnikov, a famous male ballet dancer, and Ashton's dress code included white tights, ballet shoes, and a tunic. After the book report, questions were peppered from the teacher about the famous character's imaginary home life. The teacher queried, "With all of that exercise, what do you think Mr. Baryshnikov drank to quench his thirst? Wouldn't that be the elixir of life, Ashton?" My son answered with great gravitas, sincerity, and clarity, "Wine, like at our house." It wouldn't have been such an embarrassment if he went to school in Italy or France. When I ran into that teacher twenty-five years later, she still remembered his witticism.

〰

Hi Mom
12:02 and all's well.
Wake me before you leave
please—I need to pack
Sleep Well—
Ashton

Life is filled with choices and the ramifications of those decisions. The culmination of three long middle-school years with below-average grades was a year in Florence, Italy. Was this a classic case of poor choices being rewarded? Ashton failed middle school, and he got a trip to Europe. I saw the opportunity for a fresh start, a new beginning. He was attempting to be brave at fourteen, yet he viewed the displacement from his home, family, and friends as punitive and never thought I would follow through on my threats. I knew if he weren't motivated, it could result in lifelong catastrophic consequences. I lacked the skills he desperately needed. It was all I could do to put food on the table and get the clothes washed. A school attempting to fit round pegs in square holes had resulted in his boredom and failure to produce the necessary grades to attend the high school of my dreams for him. I could figure this problem out and fix it.

Right after the divorce, I'd met Sid. He was a kind soul, and the children adored him. He was patient and wise, and he listened to them. They were drawn to the difference in parenting styles: he nurtured and cajoled appropriate behavior while I demanded and set unrealistic goals. We had a warm and loving affair, filled with hope of making a life together.

In the months before the life-changing move for Ashton was hatched, I had made a choice in my relationship with Sid. His promise to parent my children while I continued to build my business was not what I wanted. He wanted to stay home and play Nintendo with the kids, and I wanted a partner with a job outside the house. I regret my parting words to Sid about how a nanny could do the same thing. I was blunt and hurtful to a kind and generous soul. I loved him deeply, yet my desperation was palpable. Like a thirteen-year-old who vacillated weekly on the state of the world and how it could impact her contentment, I wasn't sure if I wanted a breadwinner, a father substitute, someone to save me, or a mixture of all three. Sid was honorable, and, though we were not meant to be a couple, he overcame his hurt and would remain in my children's lives. It was Sid's wise counsel I turned to when I wasn't sure what the options for Ashton's future were to be.

One month after our break-up, Sid moved to Italy to put physical distance between himself and the failed love affair. Six months later, when we were out of options for high school, Sid offered Ashton his home in Italy, his guidance through homework and schooling, and, most importantly, his heart. Instinct guided my decision that this was the correct path for Ashton, even in the face of intense scrutiny from Ashton's father and my mother. The global, life-altering year was filled with promise and the belief he could change with the strong love and guidance from a man. This was a fact that was the most difficult to accept. I could not be all things to my children.

⟨◡⟩

Good Evening—
It's 12:10 and I'm back
Please wake me for
the final day of work
Gracias
E
Buenos Noches
Ashton

Here's a piece of advice. Send them as far away as possible to learn the deepest and greatest lesson of all. And above all, don't mess with Mom.

To the defense of sixth-, seventh-, and eighth-graders world-wide, the best idea would be to build large farms with cows and sheep, greenhouses and gardens, trees and bees, and all manner of outdoor life to create an atmosphere of learning on the job. There should be cooking and cleaning classes and basic tool usage and food canning and storage classes. A store should be stocked on the premises, and a barter system set up to explain commodities and day trading. All traditional sit-down indoor classes would be banned, and there would be no grades. Peer pressure to succeed would push each child to be part of the team. A peer-based court system could sit in judgment of broken rules and promises, with everyone having a turn to be on the jury during their three years.

Traditional education places high-energy kids in classroom seats for five to seven hours a day and requires informational exchange through grading systems only, challenging short-term retention. An education surrounding life skills—how to navigate relationships and careers, financial responsibilities, and investments; how to think logically; and how to incorporate this into the real-world students will be entering upon the completion of high school—is an alternative worth exploring.

Only a few get through middle school unscathed. My idea would work. I saw my great kid dismantled in middle school. His brain wasn't engaged, and he needed to move and be physically stimulated as well as mentally challenged. By the time he wasn't accepted into the "proper" high schools, I had spent a fortune on private schools. He wasn't going to start public school as a reward for failing middle school.

Ashton learned to write because of Sid, who dusted off his English master's degree and taught Ashton how to read great books and write discussion papers. Not only had I entrusted my boy to a man halfway across the world, but I had trusted Sid would nurture the man within my boy. His father had abdicated responsibility long before, and becoming a man was not a subject with which I was well-versed.

How bad could Italy be? Think *zuppa inglese, stracciatella, tartufo, torta setteveli, baccio*; Italy is gelato heaven.

I'm sure at first it seemed pretty bad to a fourteen-year-old California boy who had been banished to a country where no one spoke his native tongue. But after three months of attempting to figure out how he was going to make it for a year not speaking to anyone, he started to pick up the language. It wasn't as difficult as he first anticipated, and that single act profoundly changed his life.

Today's world is connected, but in the 1995 it wasn't. There was a beauty, I would suppose, in the experience of foreign lands before the internet: no cell phones, no constant contact; letters, long, descriptive letters, about the world view from another country's eyes, written on a month-long ocean voyage. I was born in the wrong era besides being misplaced.

Hi—
Cinnamon's private school is a weird world
I didn't embarrass her too much, it sounded like she'd
had fun
Sleep Well
Ashton

In 1981, when I began to have my own children, I figured the best thing to do was to give them the finest education money could buy: private schools; personal coaching in sports, music, and dance; and plenty of quality time with a therapist. I was married to a man whose film company salary afforded a lifestyle in accordance with expectations of a solid economic future, which would, surely, produce happiness and prosperity. The marriage represented everything I had been taught by my mother. This worked well until the 1989 divorce and papers that took three years to be final, since he held out on signing them for that long. It was perfect—until it wasn't.

The first child followed the plan, the second got kicked out of every private school in the area, and third graduated in the bottom fifth of her high school class.

Once again, not going according to plan.

Since I fought to keep the children in the best schools, their father's lack of financial support was the final blow that torched what little feeling was left in what was supposed to be "until death do us part." As the end of our marriage arrived with its air of finality, I was coached by a therapist to say to John the actual words, "I want a divorce." It was not an easy or well-received discussion. When our reality was laid out on the table like a losing poker hand, the moment and many subsequent moments became freeing. There was no more reason to fake anything. For a brief time, the tension, strife, mental anguish, and pain we doled out to each other on a daily basis was over.

Perhaps it would have been easier if there had been a new set of arms awaiting my exit, but that didn't happen. I needed to feel the pain and be alone. I tinkered my life back together with spit and twine, treating myself as if I were recovering from major surgery. Metaphorically, a part of my body was being cut out, so it wasn't a stretch to liken this experience to surgery. It meant bed rest, plenty of healthy food and water, naps in the sunshine with the cat and dog, and the only thing to worry about was feeling better. Fat chance. Instead, I was in the hamster wheel of life. There wasn't time to rest, much less comfortably.

The divorce was the beginning of unending rounds of moving, attempting to pay bills, selling jewelry to raise the difference between the rent money coming in from the family house and the mortgage payments, and the endless pretending that everything was totally normal. We began living separate lives in 1989 and signed final divorce papers in 1993. Ours was what would come to be known as a high-conflict divorce. Fortunately, I do not suffer from a victim mentality. One year after moving from our house with four bed-rooms and three baths on an acre in downtown "Most Beautiful

Coastal City," USA, I was living in eight hundred square feet of space with three children and steadfastly refusing to unpack the boxes that would make a small living room look livable. This was not my destiny. If I avoided unpacking those boxes, it wasn't going to come true.

One afternoon, a dear friend showed up on the doorstep of said apartment and without a word began to unpack boxes. She told me, with love and concern, that it wasn't going to get any better until I faced how bad it really was, so I had better unpack those boxes and make the best of a rough situation. She helped me create a living space that had a semblance of order and a place for the four of us to be together that wasn't on a bed. I will be forever grateful to this friend.

In the years to come, there would be so much more to face, and so much more that was more difficult than unpacking a few boxes. But that first step, with the love of my friend, helped me to face the unknown with a shred of decency and hope.

There are always defining moments. Many incidents led to the end. The actual straw that broke the camel's back, or my heart, was the idea that my children would be taken out of the schools they had grown to love due to lack of finances. I was adamant about their education. Instead of private school tuition, he wanted to keep the $600 a month lease on a Lincoln Town Car.

It was a stupid Lincoln Town Car that was the defining factor and the end to a seventeen-year relationship. The car was more important than the children.

I had been left with the Corvette convertible—definitely not the most practical car with three children, though it was the car I had dreamed of as a teenager. He and I were on different planets: Planet Present vs. Glitter Galaxy. For my part, being the practical one was a new role.

He had a near-death experience a few months after my demand for a divorce while driving too fast in a rainstorm. Even the behemoth that is a Lincoln Town Car can hydroplane on a bridge. He lived to tell the story, over and over and over.

In 2011, I'd discover something I hadn't known existed before then. Dr. Ira Tukat, a highly celebrated consultant, professor, scientist, and therapist, published a report on something called Malicious Parent Syndrome. This would finally confirm for me that I was a victim, not only of my former husband, but of one of his offspring from another marriage.

Malicious Parent Syndrome is one where one parent continually debases the other parent in harmful, vengeful, purposeful, and highly reproachful ways.

Malicious Parent Syndrome is characterized by four major criteria. Someone suffering from the syndrome:

1) Attempts to punish the divorcing parent through alienating their children from the other parent and involving others or the courts in actions to separate parent and child.
2) Seeks to deny children visitation and communication with the other parent and involvement in the child's school or extracurricular activities.
3) Lies to their children and others repeatedly and may engage in violations of law.
4) Doesn't suffer any other mental disorder that would explain these actions.

Typically, this syndrome is attached to the behavior of the custodial parent. In my case, I was the recipient of this behavior as the custodial parent, and at the time no one wanted or knew how to help. I wasn't the only victim either; there were three others who suffered at the hands of a sad, jealous, and vindictive man.

Twenty-eight years after the divorce, I finally came to terms with the realities of what I'd lived through. I sometimes recall the time when a dear friend, who had been visiting for the weekend while I was still married to the kids' dad, pulled me aside and whispered in my ear, "Do you know you are a victim of verbal abuse?" I didn't have a clue. It was my normal.

As the story goes, the divorce cost more than we had. He got most everything, and I walked away, happy to be out. Somehow, I managed to keep the kids in their schools with scholarship requests and the generosity of my mother. Ashton, plagued with the responsibility of his little sister's high school social engagements due to my abdication of driving other than to work, took her to a school dance. Apparently, he was able to blend into the background enough to not cause Cinnamon total and irreversible embarrassment for being shepherded from one event to the other by her older brother. She was the only senior in her school without a driver's license because my simplistic view of raising children was to find something they loved and immerse them in it, day and night and weekends, thereby reducing the amount of time they had to get into trouble. There was no time to practice driving or take a driving exam.

Good Evening,
The full moon was spectacular
this evening.
I hope the show went well
And that you didn't leave at intermission

Sorry about Cinnamon, I thought they would
wait until at least a half hour before sunset
Sleep Well
Ashton
p.s. What's the schedule for tomorrow?

There is something about sitting through an entire *anything* that provokes my favorite line: The last half hour of anything is too long.

I had the opportunity to be a guest for an entire opera season in San Francisco at the beloved War Memorial Opera House. The program opened with Wagner's *Der Meistersinger* at a whopping five hours and fifteen minutes long. I am an opera aficionado, having been raised by an opera-adoring mother who whisked me from *Madame Butterfly* to *The Barber of Seville*. I wasn't as thrilled about that as a ten-year-old, but as I aged and realized that I had heard Beverly Sills in over six operas by the time I was fifteen, I woke up to this glorious art form and have adored the medium ever since, grateful for those early experiences.

This was the same mother—then a grandmother—who insisted that the firstborn accompany her for his first trip to Europe. The offer was super, yet it was on my mother's bucket list. I have a bucket list, too. Mine has on it to visit the best island in the world. My mother's contained an event that many are mercifully not aware even takes place. The destination was the thirty-fifth performance of the Passion Play in Oberammergau, Bavaria, Germany.

As the story goes, in 1633, the residents of this small hamlet vowed that if God spared them from the demonic and viral bubonic plague ravaging the region, they would produce a play thereafter for all time depicting the life and death of the deity who saved them from this disease. The adult death rate slowly subsided to one in the month of July 1633. The villagers believed they had been spared due to their belief in Jesus, and they kept their part of the vow. The Passion Play has been performed every decade from that time forward.

Mother, being an inveterate and convinced Catholic, wouldn't have missed the crucifixion for the world. I loved to travel and Ashton, age ten, was old enough to remember, so the three of us set our course for Germany. I am not sure I can express in words the mind-numbing eight hours of the play, not including meal breaks, that Ashton endured at age ten. He would never forget the mesmerizing effects of the birds that flew in patterns above the outdoor amphitheater. They were obviously sent by Jesus, who knew, straight up, that a ten-year-old was languishing in the audience and desperately needed diversion.

To add insult to injury, we hopped on the tour bus back to the hotel only to be informed by the perfect mother of three on the same tour that her children would love to share their reports, complete with art work, the next morning at breakfast with those of us on the bus who would enjoy such a pastime.

I could think of a way to halt her bout with perfection, yet most of my thoughts were against the law as well as all the tenets of the Passion of Christ that had been force fed to me just hours earlier. My son and I skipped breakfast the next morning. It was worth feeling hungry just to miss the incredible pomposity of Miss Matching Shoes and Handbag. The last seven and a half hours of the play served as a reminder to Ashton that it's never too late to plan your bucket list. There will be another passion play in 2020 and 2030. Don't miss out!

Grrr . . . Make sure there is coffee tomorrow morning,
or I will be grumpy. I'll rise, but I'll be damned if I'm
going to shine.
—Ashton

He did shine, and that is why there were more children. Understanding the truth that every child is different, despite having the same parents and seemingly the same upbringing, doesn't come up in conversation when you're pregnant with a second child. I didn't think there might be differences until faced with the obvious. If the easy child is first and sleeps through the night after a week, naïveté rushes in with the age-old question: how bad can Number Two really be? Parents are overcome with anticipation of the next perfect baby, so when the second child's reality is a 180 from the perfect firstborn, questions and conflict arise.

While I was pregnant with Ashton, when asked what I wanted, my standard answer was that it didn't matter. I just wanted a healthy baby. I secretly harbored a desire for a girl, so I could shop for adorable baby girl clothes, hair bows, and sparkly shoes. Besides, I knew what being a girl was all about. I didn't have the faintest idea about being a boy, what to do with them, or how to teach them man things. I don't play sports, hate camping, never made car noises as a child, and have never enjoyed getting my hands dirty even while gardening. The actual thought of a boy child was frightening enough to simply not think about. Mother's Irish mantra ran like a repeating voice of doom, "A son is a son until he takes a wife, a daughter is a daughter the rest of her life." The seeds had been planted early: a girl would be infinitely more desirable. How could you possibly go through the angst of having a boy, knowing that the end of your relationship will be the day another woman walks into his life? Though I believed Mom at the time, it came from her background as an only female child giving birth to an only female child and from the men who were in her life. Her naïve, yet deeply seated belief created my fears as well as a foundation to prove her wrong with the advent of the birth of my son, Ashton.

There is nothing quite like giving birth for the first time, regardless of the gender, and even after I recognized this was a boy child, the warnings were useless. I bonded with Ashton the moment he opened his eyes, and a wave of love swept over me that I had never imagined. I wanted to be a team, his team, Team Ashton. He was *mine*.

I was hyper-committed and showed the intensity of that commitment in specially prepared food, clothing sets with many pairs of shoes, and the one convenience: not quite natural, throw-away diapers. I might have believed I was destined to be a 1980s throwback of 1960s parenting, yet I drew the line at a diaper pail. I didn't get in on the wave of nostalgia regarding cloth diapers with numerous pails and wet bags of soaking liquids. As the story goes for many women, by the time the second child arrives, it's jars of Gerber, and the third and subsequent children eat Cheerios off the floor, happy to be fed. That certainly was the case in our household. Family was a huge help, and Grandfather J. R. read to the first two constantly. He died before he could impart his gift of time to the third.

I dove headfirst into school volunteering and became president of the Mother's Club. There was no doubt I could do it all, but it also required a tremendous amount of backup. The 1980s in California were boom times for the economy until 1988, when the real estate market crashed. Until that time we had been upwardly mobile, which meant a foreign nanny, a large home, three cars, private-school education, and dinner parties. John insisted on well-behaved, well-dressed, and thoroughly mannered children and wife. The façade was important, and Ashton innately understood from a young age how to win positive reactions from his father, which were essential to gain his affection.

When the time came when we could no longer travel together due to preschool, John would be gone for weeks at a time. My tight bond with Ashton, forged even more deeply during these times, became a liability in John's perception. He didn't mean it as a compliment but as an intended checkmark on the page of who gets what: furniture, stocks, cars, children. He only wanted the furniture, stocks, and cars. He would tolerate a weekend visit with the kids if they were well-behaved, but when one had an accident in the bed, he became livid, treating the incident as a personal affront. The first one skated outside of conflict. It wasn't until years later that I would see the challenges created by an absent father when Ashton became distant and cold around age thirteen. My sweet little boy had gone away.

Good Evening—
It's 1:15 and I am home.
I don't know what it is, but the stars are amazing tonight.
So you should look at them tomorrow as the moon will
still be very faint.
—Ashton

Regardless of my lack of information and most especially nuances on the subject, it was now my job to coach my boy into manhood.

This would encompass the subject of sex. I wanted to help him, but my desire was different from my ability. I knew the intimacy of a sexual conversation might breed contempt or embarrassment for both the parent and the teenager, and that no one would emerge unscathed. I figured fourteen would be the perfect age, yet I waited—I'm not sure for what. By the time Ashton was almost sixteen, the time for that conversation had expired.

I didn't consciously or intentionally ignore the subject, and at one point I had a talk in the car on the way to school about the importance of paying attention to what a date was saying, respecting the word no, and being a gentleman. My thoughts were approaching sex and its behaviors, yet the words didn't find their way out of my head—or the traffic light changed colors, and I was absolved due to time constraints. I already considered myself halfway down the crazy road attempting to keep everyone on the straight and narrow, scraping together money for groceries and gas, and keeping a home that didn't look like a halfway house for orphaned minors. Why couldn't his father or some other male figure step up to this conversation? My instinct was to look for a savior, someone smarter and more adept, someone to take over because I was tired, bone tired, of doing it all and not comfortable with a subject I wasn't entirely sure of myself. I didn't know how to explain an erection popping up solely because the homecoming queen visited your algebra class to talk about volunteering to decorate the gym. I didn't realize or want to believe it should all be on my shoulders.

While Ashton, by my expectation, should have been anxious to date and have sex, he befriended many young women, rarely bringing them home for anything more than an hour or two of music and talk. I left them to their lives and didn't demand they be in plain sight. His room was his bastion of self, and I didn't believe in holding him to the standards I had grown up with: no opposite sex folk in the bedroom. Seemed silly to me when any place would work for an encounter, so why make one room off-limits? To clarify, when I was in junior high, my parents gave away my four-poster bed to make room for twin beds, turning the room into an L-shaped sofa/sectional sitting room with large pillows and bolsters, so the connotation of conversation pit, rather than bed, was conveyed to my visitors.

What no one told me was that you not only worry if your son or daughter is having sex, you worry if they *aren't* having sex. And then there were questions of sexual orientation. I wouldn't be the parent, should one of my children announce sexual tendencies outside the heterosexual realm, to run screaming from the room, yet I wanted know one way or the other so I could check that one off and move on to the next issue. I was a list maker and a journaler and considered it to be a measure of my competence when things were done, fixed, finished. Then it was time to move on to the next project. Child-rearing fell under the project heading: one issue fixed and on to the next. Ashton kept us all guessing for a while, and being emotionally and sexually insecure myself, I simply couldn't ask him if he thought he was gay. It was difficult coming out of a seventeen-year marriage, and at thirty-six years old, I hadn't had many sexual experiences myself.

I believed I had to be everything, and that included a perceived power base that was strong and impenetrable, wise and knowledgeable. Children look to their parents for guidance. What Ashton got as a role model was a naïve and stoic mother who attempted to successfully be both mother and father. I wanted to believe his sensitivity was something I fostered by my terrific parenting skills, yet he was his own person. His vulnerability was built on abandonment. It's difficult to trust and share after your world has been ripped apart. Although he appeared to be just fine and scoffed at my prying questions, no one is fine when one biological parent chooses not to be in your life. There is fallout. It simply takes time to manifest itself.

In the misguided belief that I could fill all the roles necessary and be the driving force behind successful children, I placed a tremendous pressure on my fragile psyche. Resiliency after divorce comes only with facing the reality of what has happened, where you are now, and, most importantly, how to move forward. Those tough questions, at the time too frightening to even ask, remained unanswered, just like the topic of the birds and the bees.

Dear Parents,
I'm afraid that early turned to late, and late turned
to delirium,
so at 11:40, a tail-dragging tired boy turns in.
—Ashton

An old man at seventeen? Tired at 11:40?

Children don't ever seem to want to sleep. They are afraid they are going to miss all the good times. They want to push sleep as far away as possible, and they don't have the same glorious routine as we adults have established for ourselves. We brush our teeth because we want to, wash our face because we should, don comfy soft clothes, and look lovingly at the big puffy bed we left, lo those too many hours ago.

Children don't share the same rituals, yet if they don't get enough sleep, they will have meltdowns, exhibit the inability to play independently, be defiant, have more tantrums, lose their appetite, and be more hyperactive. We just wind down; they wind up and out the window.

I never knew what tired was until I had children. Interrupted sleep is considered a positive experience from the moment the pregnant body reaches six months and the urge to use the bathroom visits you every hour on the hour. This test is merely getting you ready for the next twenty years, give or take a few, of sleep deprivation.

Good Evening, 11:30.
The play was very well done and quite humorous.
It was a little scary to be back at my old alma mater, but I managed to avoid most of the annoying former classmates.
Sleep Well,
—Ashton

Ashton was home for a visit, which included a weekend of festivities at his old high school. He was nervous about his return to the once-hallowed halls and seeing classmates and teachers after five years of university. His experiences of living and working in the UK and France gave him a global perspective that could be, to his peers, at once fascinating to absorb and easily construed (albeit unintentionally on his part) as haughty and condescending. The latter might have had something to do with his evolving British accent, adopted from his new home. On a pragmatic level and because his graduating class was quite small, he knew everyone. But five years had passed, and Ashton had changed more than his classmates in many ways. This vital leap in growth—leaving home and studying for what would be ostensibly your life's work—also creates a set of higher stakes for all kids; the ego wishes to be accepted and perhaps admired for accomplishments and maturity.

He went to a high school without a set dress code. The laissez-faire California attitude adopted by the administration regarding standards for clothing fostered a climate that served the same purpose. Likeminded individuals, forming groups based on their mutual interests, unified and defined themselves by their daily wear. His group of burgeoning philosophers, budding intellectuals, and aspiring authors leaned toward military-issue, steel-toed, high-laced, jet-black boots, hunter green raincoats, undone buttons, and flowing coattails flapping in the wind, creating a surreal collage of flightless birds desperately attempting liftoff yet not possessing the vital aerodynamic capabilities. His group leaned toward Nintendo and fencing, Sartre and Kierkegaard, and believed in the portrayal of life as dismal angst. It was only after a couple of trips from the US to the UK and being detained at the security gate due to the steel-toed shoes that he reinvented his look to an open collared shirt and pants that actually fit his trim figure. It could have been maturity, yet I was compelled not to mention that possibility.

I learned from him after that evening that former mentors and teachers relished updates and accomplishments. Classmates eased into the conversation cautiously at first, inhibitions soon replaced with shared memories and laughter. Ashton proved he could be an adult for an evening visit. Good impressions were created, some past conflicts forgotten, and a dawning realization apparently appeared that change is not necessarily something to be feared. The instructors saw more in him than he did and were a part of his life—and that it was not all bad.

NO PAPER = QUICK NOTE
All is well
11:52
See you bright and early
Sleep Well
—Ashton

This note, written on the tiniest scrap, let me know that there must not have been any paper in the immediate vicinity. Ashton, like a lot of kids, wouldn't have looked beyond his nose to find something adequate to write on. Clearly it was my responsibility to make sure those materials existed, set up and waiting for him—with the proper writing utensil—upon walking through the front door. It was another detail in which I was at fault, of which I would be reminded on numerous occasions for years to come. In an attempt to understand mothering and the guilt associated with the job when you realize the directions don't come with the child, I've found that there are six types of mothers:

1) Perfectionist. Hand in hand with this goes high expectations and a general orientation to deem children guilty until proven innocent.
2) Unpredictable. This was *my* mother.
3) Best Friend. I see the fallout from this type of mothering daily.
4) Me First. There's something wrong with this one?
5) Guilty.
6) Complete. Seriously? This one is just tacked on for good measure. I've never met one.

From an early age, my perfectionism propelled Ashton's maniacal desire to remind me of where I had fallen short, made an error, or left one of the kids at the soccer field or a dance lesson. I wanted perfect children, so, in turn, I had to be the perfect parent. That concept was trashed upon realizing even my perfect children had temper tantrums and created scenes out of Dante's seventh circle of hell on a regular basis.

Had I been less than Teflon-coated, I would have caved. Here I was attempting to do my best at every turn—well, at least at most turns—and then you have the firstborn smarty pants ripping through your adult façade and gloating in his perceived independence from the parent, though certainly a necessary step in the formation of a functioning adult. In many ways, mothering is a strange and wonderful occupation. When you think about it, we are gifted or cursed (depending upon the moment) with the opportunity to grow a live human being into a productive adult, armed with all of the knowledge and wisdom we can download into them during eighteen years.

On the surface it seems easy, yet it's the most difficult, trying, joyful, heartbreaking, and everything in between task imaginable. Then, they go away and, for a time, don't look back. All we can do is hope our tenets of kindness to all, having a humble attitude, and maintaining the desire to be the best we can be stay with them through their trials. We cannot save them from pain and hurt, yet parental love should build a buffer to inhumanity and give the strength to do what is right in the face of tough times. Perhaps the most important thing we give our children is the knowledge that when we all make a wrong decision, which we all do from time to time, love is never conditional. Parental love will be there through heartaches, pain, and inevitable downturns.

I was simply trying to control my children so that they would have blissfully happy lives when they grew up. It's easy to control a one-year-old or a two-year-old. You just pick them up and tell them what to do. Teenagers are so hard because they keep asking, "why, why?" and saying that things aren't fair and bringing to attention all your flaws and pointing out your mistakes.

~⌣~

Good Evening—
You know . . . I say I'm going to
be out late, but I forgot
that I have nothing to do
in Monterey, so here I am, back
at 11:03.
Gah.
—Ashton

They roamed the streets of an adjacent small town, mostly because there were fast food joints that were not allowed in Fairytale Land where we resided. Trench coats with tails flying in the breeze and coarse black steel-toed boots were the dress code, male or female, and, despite any weather change or dry cleaning necessity, the uniform set them apart from the wandering tourists and high school students from other schools. They hung out in these prepackaged groups, sharing the same elitist private school education, personal vehicles, and wide open curfews created to maximize the outward belief there was total trust—until there wasn't. It's not easy to get alcohol when you're underage, so the local coffee shop became the respite from the rain and boredom of the street. I often pondered the possibility of naming rights for the tables at the locally owned java spot and quietly thanked the owners for allowing the kids to congregate and not seeing them as a menace. Teenagers are driven by dissatisfaction, and this group was no different from the teenagers in Mobile, Alabama, or Mars, Pennsylvania. Age limits choices, and the high school age is too old for many activities and too young for others.

Most of the regulars in Ashton's gang had siblings, and along with that came the opportunity to make a few dollars babysitting said siblings. It did occasionally take away from a weekend night on the street.

One Saturday afternoon and evening when he was around fifteen, Ashton was watching his younger brother and sister while I attended a nearby event with Reg.

Thirty minutes into the event, the sheriff arrived to inform us they had received a call from a neighbor and been dispatched to our home. It seems the neighbor thought Ashton was attempting to drown his younger brother in the pool and had created such a ruckus that the authorities were now on-site. My initial thought was unless someone was dead, they were going to be looking forward to a tortuous existence in the next few weeks. After hurrying home, I ascertained the drama was without bloodshed or fluid-filled lungs and that they'd just been having fun. Once the parental units' blood pressure levels had self-corrected, we left for the remainder of the event. All was quiet on the home front when we returned later that evening.

One of the most difficult things to achieve with Ashton, and in general while parenting, was to arrive at an enforceable consequence for inappropriate behavior. It was different being a teenager for children in the '80s and later, at least from my memory of teenage years. The social pressure as well as the pressure to achieve in school is palpable and could have sent Ashton over a waterfall, but the near-drowning event was one of only a few negative instances of attempting to find an alternative to typical teenage boredom.

❧

Late night—3:20 am
It was fun . . . sorry about the time
Love you
—Ashton

In a word, the most important thing to teenagers is *freedom*. The question of curfews arises for several reasons. Parents are terrified of the night and their teenagers running wild, and kids pull the trust card. I remember my mother's mantra, one of many: "Nothing good ever happens after 10 p.m." I was a wild high school child, so I had a female perspective on what can go on when the sun sets. My memory with my own kids is that I fell into the unequal and dysfunctional parenting trap: no curfew for the boys, yet later I imposed a curfew on Cinnamon.

It was my observation that Ashton didn't need a curfew because he had lived in Europe at age fourteen. Since he'd survived that, he was done with a need for parental controls. He had been under the supervision of a strong male figure for a year, so that part of my parenting responsibility had been handed over, taken care of, accomplished. His summer job as a techie with a local classical summer music festival kept him out until the early morning hours. I am sure work was over by midnight, yet having lived my life in theatre, I realized it takes a couple of hours to readjust after a show and let the excitement of live theatre wane. He was working in a field I understood and I was familiar with the rules of live theatrical production, so the late hours didn't concern me.

My permissive attitude toward Ashton, despite how strongly I felt about raising nonsexist children in the 1980s, still carried the conditioning from how I was parented. Some of my parenting style stems from a parent's number one worst fear for a teenage high school daughter: getting pregnant. Getting someone pregnant ranks ninth on the list for parents of boys. The notion that I was going to curb pregnancy with a curfew is utterly ridiculous. I am grateful Cinnamon did not get pregnant in high school, and the boys never got anyone pregnant, either.

Fear-based standards were right up my mental alley. I figured boys could get themselves out of a compromising situation, fight back, stand up for themselves verbally, and generally not need protection. So, I permitted Ashton to stay out until three thirty in the morning when the job defined the hours, with only a mild reprimand, even though I lay awake in the wee hours willing his safe return and the soft whoosh of a note under my door.

All Hail the Conquering Hero—1:40 am
Sorry about the time, but
I so very nicely won the croquet
match that I didn't
want to come home before
we were finished.
With skill and strategy befitting an international
croquet master, I came from second to last and by
exploiting the foolish squabbles between first and
second place, managed to secure a victory.

Then they worked a rematch, but I decided I need to sleep.
Sleep, ahhh . . . and the police presence in small town USA
is scary, so I drove extra slow.
Oh well,
—Ashton

Croquet at one in the morning, along with placement on the university fencing team—not your typical football Saturday afternoon with a beer-laden tailgate picnic. Ashton's education was definitely not of the US variety. His love of croquet and fencing made for interesting conversations among friends.

Croquet is credited with being the first Olympic sport in which women participated, but the game's tenure was limited to a one-time-only appearance in Paris 1900. Only French competitors signed up for the event, and only a single spectator purchased a ticket to see it.

Aside from the constant flow of new factoids delivered from a student across the pond, Ashton's most important comment in the note under the door was not wanting to stop before finishing. And all this from the self-avowed President of the Perpetual Procrastinators' Professional Society. Guess it is easier to procrastinate on a term paper than a winning sports event, and it's always easier to get more pleasurable little things done than big scary ones.

What did I expect from his $100,000 education? I'm not sure, but Croquet Master? All hail indeed!

This is the child who, if you asked what time it was, would tell you how the watch was made. We call him Professor Ashton: a connoisseur of fine cheeses, a dabbler in fencing, an avowed procrastinator, and now a croquet god.

How on earth can three children be so different from one

another? Genes are not the only reason siblings are different. If you know any identical twins, you'll know they are definitely different people even though they share the exact same genes.

Where personality is concerned, it's also important to remember that things like a child's social and family environment and relationships play an important role.

Children will have different relationships due to things such as being in different schools and having different hobbies and habits. The environment also includes their relationships with their siblings, and of course, birth order.

Personality-wise, most siblings will be more alike to one another than to a random stranger, but not too much more alike.

With my three kids, the first child got the most attention and the most privileges. That said, we loved them all differently. Darwin labeled divergence as a main player in familial siblings' differences. I saw this. The first child excelled at the piano, while the second child was unable or unwilling to compete. He instead became a social butterfly. Ashton, the firstborn, was a parental pleaser, conscientious and respectful of authority, as witnessed in the comment about driving more slowly with the police cars in sight. The second assumed an alternative reality. The wild child— the third child—often got called the dog's name, probably due to all the chaos.

This small village watched out for its children, and the police presence was one I appreciated on more than one occasion. A small town is full of watchful eyes, some peering where they are not wanted and some necessary for safety. Such was the police force in our coastal town. When they combined with the local newspaper to print the police log, those who had erred against a city law had the sting of seeing their names emblazoned in black and white for all to regard and slowly shake their heads, actually pleased their name was not included in the print of shame.

Ashton's midnight mallet madness set the log afire with gossip and fueled his reputation as a gaming man. The Croquet Master had been caught but was not to be convicted.

Good Evening—12:10
Late night, Denny's for ice cream.
Didn't like the atmosphere—
just for future reference, if you
want ice cream late one night,
Safeway would be a better choice.
—Ashton

The atmosphere at Denny's? Food, its preparation and degustation, had always been a huge part of Ashton's life. I loved to cook, and Ashton liked to be in the kitchen surrounded by great cooking smells, attractively arranged tables, and friends and family enjoying a meal. His distaste for Denny's atmosphere could have been construed as snobbery, the result of a having spent so much time in Europe, first in Italy for a single year abroad in high school and later in the UK for six years of university education, yet I know it started long before he left for school. He was raised a foodie before the term was popular, and our family life had always been connected to the dining room table.

The fact that Ashton announced on his first trip back to the States freshman year, at the baggage claim no less, that he was now an avowed vegetarian, was a shocking big deal, especially since a rack of lamb was awaiting his return, marinating in olive oil and rosemary in the fridge. A heads up would have been thoughtful. His reasons were understandable once explained. It was 2000, and since 1993 there had been over 180,000 reported bovine infections of mad cow disease. In 1998, one year before his education in Britain began, the European Union banned all meat for sale from the UK. This turn of events, a detour in the epicurean road, triggered recipes with vegetarian ideas, though I was daunted by tofurky and only made it once. After resounding cries of angst from the tasting committee, it was deemed inedible and tossed in the trash.

That year, the spring of Ashton's freshman year, Reg and I took the other two children to visit London and Ashton's university. We decided on a tour at a nearby castle before lunch. Attacking the restaurant section of Fodor's, the firstborn read reviews of local specialty restaurants aloud to a family that travels on their stomachs—simply stated, foodie talk discussion of future meals while consuming the current repast. Breakfast had been hearty, yet not enough to prevent a lively discussion regarding the merits of Loch Fyne crab Marie Rose, tartar of roast veal, or tomato and crab mayonnaise, as well as the combined need to save room for the cheese course and a small sweetie. We debated the Orkney lobster ravioli versus the Shetland monkfish or roast breast of Goosnargh duck. Four hours after lunch started, we ditched all hope of visiting the castle and gave in to the riotous pleasure of a memorable meal.

The following day, we set out for the castle once again. When the three cried for lunch, I produced homemade sandwiches. We saw the castle that day. I would have preferred lunch out again, yet we managed to reminisce about a salty potato chip—or UK crisps—dessert, dipped in a generous portion of soft serve vanilla ice cream as a potential ending to the soon-to-be finished bag lunches. Denny's Grand Slam Special was a dim memory.

~~~

I'm off to be a silly
young man.
I'm paranoid, so I'll be careful (12:50 am)
—Ashton
P.S. I'll leave another note when I get back in.

Ashton was rarely silly. Silly is reserved for the second child or third, but not the first.

The fact is that children change and grow, we hope. But I wasn't privy to the silly side of Ashton. He hid this personality trait until a situation arose that I viewed one way and Ashton clearly interpreted differently.

While on vacation in the south of France—another seemingly snobby comment from a university student, yet the proximity of diverse countries when living abroad makes travel very easy—Ashton texted me about how wonderful his ocean swim was going. I hadn't known he was even on vacation, and, after he failed to return my replies to him, I became worried. After numerous attempts to call him, a text came through, saying: "Chill Dude, havin' fun."

As far as I knew, this type of "bro speak" had never passed my firstborn's lips. I was certain he had been kidnapped, his cell phone stolen, and the ransom note imminent—or he was dead. Given to drama and its ensuing panic attacks, I called the phone company and reported the phone stolen. I was paying for the service, so they complied and cancelled the service. A day later I got a text from Ashton from an unknown phone number asking why his phone was not in service. I called and reinstated the service and didn't tell him that I thought "Chill Dude" was not an appropriate greeting for his mother.

The other incident happened when, as a third-year university student, Ashton lived on the third floor of an ancient dorm overlooking a golf course in the blustery weather Scotland is known to produce. I was grateful he accepted my weekly phone calls, and therefore started feeling concerned when a week and few days had passed without his acknowledging my messages. My conscious mind told me that if he were dead, the school would let me know, yet I could see him, in his dorm room, dying from a mysterious disease and no one being any the wiser. I did the only thing a mother in the same position would have done. I called the president of the school. Explaining my story at length, the proper British administrator promised to find my boy and have him return my calls. A frosty phone call came a few hours later. I had to promise on my life that I would never again commit such an atrocity.

I promised, yet I had made my point.

3:30 am.
Home, safe and unaffected by paranoia.
Just don't ask me what we did. . . .
—Ashton (accompanied by a hand-drawn mouth
dripping with blood)

Today's term *helicopter parent* hadn't been coined in the late '90s, yet apparently someone had channeled my chakras and created the category. I couldn't be at every soccer game, debate team rehearsal, or field hockey tournament, but I could certainly worry the issues to death on a regular basis. I lived through a horrendous bike accident involving untied shoelaces and an emergency visit to the dental surgeon, ER visits with 105-degree fevers, car wrecks, failing grades, and heartbroken love affairs. Paranoid Patty, their nickname for me, did reduce Ashton's interest in sharing events as they happened.

A few years after a beach outing, he was feeling remorseful regarding his ineptitude at being a good caretaker and role model. He had ventured, with his siblings, far beyond the shallow shore of a swimming beach where they were frolicking and still within my vision. Lulled into a false sense of security, I had either drifted off to sleep (or been more interested in my lovely pink adult beverage with its tiny umbrella perched on the rim) and missed seeing how very far they had floated, swam, and played away from shore. Attempting not to panic and to be the brave big brother, Ashton cajoled, pulled, and generally saved the smaller children I was blissfully ignoring, since he was so competent and trustworthy. He'd sworn his siblings to secrecy, so I didn't find out about the tale of the perilous journey to safety with potentially dreadful possibilities until years later.

I didn't have to ask what he did in this note. Sometimes it is better not to know. On second thought, it's usually better not to know.

～ၖ⌒

Good Evening, 3:13. And as always,
Bach keeps me out late.
It was fortuitous that the
heavens cleared especially for Bach.

The stars were magnificent and
it wasn't too chilly.
Feel free to let me sleep in tomorrow as Saturday is
a big work night.
Yeah, he's a pretty cool guy if you ask me.
Sleep Well
—Ashton

I wonder if Bach's mother thought he was a pretty cool guy.

Ashton grew up with a real-life backstage experience, when I wasn't insisting he be on stage in tights and ballet shoes. He enjoyed the technical side of production. Until middle school ended, he humored me with onstage appearances and took pleasure in the team approach to presenting dances choreographed around the one boy in class. He shared tough times and insensitive name calling and bullying at school regarding his participation in my world of ballet, which was largely concentrated in the third grade.

The ungrounded stereotypical assertion that ballet would make boys gay was a falsehood fostered by many of the fathers of his classmates. Homophobia is hardwired into our culture, but I encouraged my boys when it came to ballet. As dancers progressed, they were placed in a specific class teaching the fundamentals of partnering the ballerina. This class allowed for holding the female dancer in lifts and promenades, with hands and arms wrapped around her limbs and torso, something not fostered in other arenas. On this particular class day, a plethora of the dancers' admirers would sit on an outside bench peering into the classroom, wishing they could trade places with Ashton.

His understanding of theatre from both backstage and onstage gained him an exceptional summer job for the four years he was enrolled in university. He was introduced to some of the finest musicians in the world who played during our local month-long festival in celebration of classical music. His friendship with one of the directors led him to a relationship with the daughter of one of the visiting musicians and introduced him to his first summer of love—and his first crushing breakup as summer waned.

Bach was a very cool guy in our household, and, in time with one of his concertos, all three children would practice pirouettes in the kitchen while I made dinner. That was normal in our household. They expressed their individuality and recognized early the power of creativity. They supported each other in the dance classroom and had uproarious conversations about backstage preteen gossip. They recognized it took a team to produce a show. When I needed a sound man, Scooter stepped in; when I needed someone to change sets, Ashton was there; and when I didn't ask for an opinion, Cinnamon offered hers. The family that dances together builds lasting and strong relationships together.

I'm home (12:27)
One more sad good-bye. Wake me early
to pack.
Summers go too quickly
Sunsets go too quickly
A precursor to life.
Love you
—Ashton

"Goodbyes are the tears of growth."
—*Ashton, original quote*

It didn't occur to me as Ashton grew from an independent elementary school student in navy blue shorts and uniform red polo shirt to a morose middle school student that what I should be teaching him was how to leave me and the comfort of his birth home to succeed in the world of university and the stark realities beyond. I also didn't understand leaving would be harder on me than on him. Raising three children alone meant going through each day in survival mode, and that didn't allow for vital self-reflection. My reactions to situational issues were ground out in gritty moments from waking to exhausted sleep.

When the time came to pack him off for university, I thought to myself, *How bad can this be?* Well, it was pretty bad. I cried every day for weeks. I am a closet crier—not actually in the closet, but in the shower, which washes away more tears than pillowcases. No one knew about these private moments of self-pity. In general, if I ever cry in front of anyone, there is something terribly, terribly wrong.

Ashton, like many other high school seniors, had one foot out the door for months before graduation and never looked back. His healthy outlook was positive reinforcement that I had done my job in at least one aspect of child-rearing. I had guaranteed his freedom, backed by a relatively intact ego and with a solid, ready to conquer the world attitude.

Ashton's original quote, "Goodbyes are the tears of growth," is a reminder of the truth that our children come through us, and they are not just for us or extensions of our misplaced desires. It was time for him to go, and it was time for me to let him go.

~⌇~

Hi,
Silly Things Accomplished
all's well that ends well.
Sweet Dreams,
—Ashton

There's a Swedish proverb I love that reads: "Small children, small worries. Big children, big worries."

There is a connection between a mother and her child that is different from other relationships. It isn't just about love.

In 2012, *Scientific American* would publish a report about how babies' cells live on in their mothers' bodies. Mixing of cells is not uncommon and is seen in bone marrow transplant recipients. Chimerism, this mixing of cells, was first noted in the UK in 1953. The woman, known only known as "Mrs. McK," gave blood at a donation drive. When the blood was tested, it was found to have two separate blood types. At the time that was thought to be biologically impossible. The mystery was solved by two leading UK physicians. The woman was a twin. The twin's blood had infused in her body while they were still *in utero*, and remained there some thirty years later.

This feeds my argument about our bond to our children being more than just love. It's a biological connection, and parts of our children do forever reside in the mother's body. Mothers are charged with the emotional responsibility and power to influence the next generation. As a single parent, I recognized the vital importance of mothering, but also the number one stressor for single moms—the financial burden—which also contributed to the number two stressor, missing being with my children. I wanted to be at the soccer games and give out Capri Suns to their teammates. I wanted to be a classroom parent responsible for celebrations and appreciation days for teachers. I was sad to have a career that, out of necessity, took me away from my own children and had me spending most of my day mentoring other people's children. There was resentment from my children. They claimed to understand that I had to work fourteen hours a day to make ends almost meet, and they claimed to know I loved them as deeply; yet many times, especially on those nights while awaiting the note under the door, I questioned every decision I made and cursed many of my choices.

Summer is gone
It's day frozen over
in the cold wind of fall
I'm home and thawing
it's 12:28
Sleep Warm
—Ashton

In the third grade Ashton was dubbed the Renaissance man, a person with many interests and much knowledge. His early years were consumed with my nurturing his whims. When he wanted to swim, I found the best coach for private lessons; when he showed aptitude for music, he studied piano with the finest. His discoveries, whether be it a random butterfly or worms dug from the earth, were as fantastic a trove of treasures as if I had never seen a Monarch myself. His first time was my first time though his eyes.

I had known I wanted children since I was a child, and the reality of years of infertility created a situation in which Ashton himself, much as I had been, became a PFB, a Precious First Baby.

It is an arguable fact that a PFB is a thing. Ask any truthful mother, and she will have to agree that the first child is treated differently from subsequent children. I admit to it. Because we shared similar birth orders, we became a team. Four years of being a single child with an absentee father created a bond. Expectations were higher because more of me was given. I had the time and energy to give my all, even when I didn't heed the wisdom of elders who said to sleep when the baby sleeps. I was young and demanded perfection from myself. I was busy expressing milk, so dairy didn't touch his lips until he was two years old. I was so worried about obesity that I made sure he didn't eat sugar. If I had known that it was OK to calm down and enjoy the baby instead of attempting to control his life and diet from birth, it would have been a much less stressful start to his life for both of us. First babies are the test pattern for new parents, and subsequent children have a much easier go of it.

⁓

Hi Mom,
I'm home safely—no further car problems
12:40
Sleep well
And I'll see you in the morning
—Ashton

Dubbed "Social Death," the car, a 1971, cherry-red, Cadillac Eldorado with white interior and padded plush top, was a gift from his grandmother. Picture a sixteen-year-old in his uniform of army green trench coat and steel-toe boots, with a candy cane car.

My mother thought the car should be immortalized, and in its own way it would be. If the car had had a voice, it would have cried to be at home in Palm Springs, California, or Del Rey Beach, Florida, or a Del Webb subdivision in the scorching summers outside of Phoenix, Arizona. It would have been at home with a seventy-year-old guy with dyed black hair, an unbuttoned shirt, and one too many gold chains around his neck, arm casually out the open driver's side window and hair unmoving in the wind. He would have the 8-track blaring with "That Old Black Magic" and be seen polishing the silver-plated fenders and checking his teeth in the sheen for leftover lunch.

Yet, it ended up with Ashton. It was parked, each school morning, as far away from the main hall as possible. The mortification surrounding "Social Death" did not stop him from a daily drive, nor did it preclude friends on the weekend. He kept it somewhat clean and tidy, yet when the time came, and the repair costs exceeded an intelligent decision to keep it in the family, there weren't many tears when it was donated to a nonprofit organization benefitting children. The car had been faithful for three years, and I didn't witness any long-term or visible emotional scarring from his less-than-perfect ride.

Hi Mom—
12:05 and I'm home.
Thanks for being somewhat
tactful about the trencher
and hood . . . was it really

that terrible? We guys
have no fashion sense.
Give me the verdict in the
morning.
Sleep Well
—Ashton

My mother used the term when I wasn't doing what she thought was best for me—it was "just a phase." I must have had a lot of phases, as I heard that term weekly.

Those folks who study such things say there are seven stages of human life. A stage is different from a phase. A phase, as my mother might have defined it, was "a testing ground for parents' sanity" or "attempting something new just to irritate the parents."

His military green trencher phase preceded "saggers," the baggie, butt-showing, low rider jeans and shorts. I will take the trench coat and the steel-toe boots over plumber's reveal any day.

There is nothing new about adults thinking young people's clothing taste is horrid. I was a product of an original 1960s, part your long hair down the middle and hold it in place with a braided leather wreath, hippie girl phase. This was much to the consternation of my cashmere twinset mother.

In the 1970s, when I met and married my children's father, fashion was rife with men in one-piece jumpsuits. This was not a good phase for many.

There was a phase in the 1980s, fostered by exercise icon Jane Fonda when my kids were young, in which bright colored leg warmers topped off with matching headbands were all the rage. And who could forget MC Hammer pants—that cross between Scheherazade and King Tut? The only reason they looked good on MC Hammer was because of his upper body, which was always shown bare and offset the ridiculous and voluminous pants.

I was also a victim of the '80s phase of all things shoulder pads.

There were phases that had my best friends hanging on every word each other spoke, dressing as twins, and believing they couldn't live without each other. Stages and phases help us understand and name the complexities of life, finding humor in defining change and growth. I am afraid the leg warmer/spandex phase alongside the male jumpsuits did not create affection or many fond remembrances. I have turned into my mother. Cue the twinset.

Dear Mom,
I want to apologize for last night.
I directly and knowingly disobeyed you
and wanted to say I was sorry for that.
I've done some thinking since them and have
decided that I need to accept and execute
my responsibilities. As a gesture of apology and
as a symbolic commitment of my new
attitude, I cleaned the kitchen, oven, and microwave,
and watered the plants.
—Ashton

Reminds me of a Zen proverb: "Experience this moment to its fullest."

Zen didn't add, "Because it may never happen again."

Taking personal responsibility for behavior that is less than exemplary shows care and awareness of how actions can be hurtful and, at times, harmful. In learning from mistakes, mature growth is fostered. When our children are young, we tell them (after getting down to their eye level), "Say you are sorry for hurting Johnny's feelings." The child says, "Sorry," and we move on. Many times, the word *sorry* doesn't equate in a youngster's mind as much as the fact that their adult has taken the time to speak with them in a tone they know is saved for times when the dog poops on the living room carpet. The terse and tense attempt-to-be-calm attitude elicits the desire to make the adult happy, so nine times out of ten, the child repeats the word and life moves on as if nothing happened.

With teenagers, not only is *I'm sorry* difficult, its precursor is what the rationally thought-out outcome will be should they choose not to apologize. When teens can focus enough out of their own thoughts to understand there are others in the world around them and really see what they've done that's caused the problem, you just might have a chance at an apology. More importantly, they might glimpse a reality in which they aren't at the center of the universe. I never expected an unprompted apology from my kids, and most of the time I wasn't surprised. Given my creed that expectations kill relationships, I was thrilled with his note about the clean kitchen, microwave, oven, and watered plants, and believed a barrier had been broken and understanding prevailed.

The last supper?
Pumpkin Pie
Quinoa (I'd like to try that)
no tofu
not sure about the rest
I'm home, sad to say good-bye
to Roberta—she leaves tomorrow as well
Sleep Well
—Ashton

In the hurried years of child-rearing, I never stopped to consider the inevitability of each one of the kids leaving the nest. Life was, on many days, a struggle to exist and not focus on the vital nuances of how important it was to be physically present and give them my time. Time was the fleeting commodity I couldn't harness enough of to support the family and nourish that which was vital to their emotional well-being. By the time Ashton went to university, there was a brief sigh of relief—one out the door and two to go. True, I cried nearly every day he was gone for the first few weeks, but the fact that he was thriving made it all bearable. Yet, on the rare occasion when all three were home and upstairs asleep in their beds, I could let go. There was an infinite peace I could pinpoint within my core. Whether true or not at that moment, I felt safe. In the late night, when I saw the notes under the door and I knew they were tucked in, I could release fear and anxiety, at least until the next day.

Scooter

....

Scooter: May 8, 1985

- By age three, defined by his waist-length blond hair
- Brown eyes
- Middle child
- Good mediator, compromiser, peacemaker
- Understood from early on that life isn't fair
- Free spirit

....

"Your older sibling is already the smart one, so the pressure's off!"
—*Scooter*

10:57
I'm home
Thanx for letting
me go
Love,
—Scooter

Forever the middle child, Scooter was the one who almost did me in. His suicide attempt at twelve was the culmination of years of frustration, tears, pills, doctors, therapists, and all types of well-wishing friends' counsel. His depression was profound, yet not linked to recreational drugs or alcohol. His abandonment issues and attention-seeking behavior coupled with my inconsistent parenting discipline resulted in an addiction to gaming, which was something he gravitated toward to stop the pain of isolation and the psychological trauma caused by abandonment. Not only had he been left behind by his father, but I was also gone from the home. A series of babysitters couldn't be expected to hold the line on behavior, help with homework, get everyone to afterschool lessons, fix dinner, and keep the peace. The broken family unit resulting from my long hours away from home and a nonexistent father figure for ten years left Scooter to raise himself. His teachers were video games and the *Terminator* movie series. By the time I told Scooter he couldn't watch that type of violence, he could recite the entire film verbatim. I also banned *The Exorcist*, but again I was too late. Left alone, he recreated scenes from the movie to frighten his younger sister, in perfect dialogue, word for word.

He had been his father's favorite. John was sixty-one at the time of Scooter's birth. We were talking divorce during what we thought were private moments, yet late-night arguments are never solitary. Children know, even if they cannot understand.

Scooter was a wild child, the antithesis of his studious and proper older brother, Ashton. John wouldn't and couldn't discipline this child; he thought him the reincarnation of himself and delighted in Scooter's defiance. I set limits and then left for work, imagining the rules would magically be obeyed.

As a young child, Scooter's rebellion was prefaced with an angelic smile that belied the behavior that followed. I knew to beware of the smile; something was up, and it was only a matter of time before he would outwit me.

When he was three, we were all at a family outing at the local pool—Dad, Ashton, Scooter, Cinnamon, and me. I told Scooter he couldn't go in the pool without me and that I would only be a moment getting my suit on in the locker room. I distinctly reiterated this, scooching to his level, telling him we would be going in the shallow end of the pool and pointing out the difference to him. As soon as I turned my back to pick up my swim bag, he was gone, full speed ahead and flying into the deep end of the pool. I saw his action in slow motion, his bright smile reflecting his delight in his abject disobedience. He had scarcely hit the water when I was I behind him, dragging him out of pool to safety. This appeared to have been a test for John and me. For a moment, Scooter had his answer, and we had passed: he was loved by two parents who were on the verge of divorce.

As he entered preschool and then kindergarten, his attention seeking drove his behavior, and his teachers and administration were not amused. He was inherently loving and adorable, but also incorrigible and impossible to control. He soon developed a reputation as a troublemaker. Though his peers adored his slightly naughty ways, their parents became wary. Mothers worried his behavior might sprinkle seeds of disobedience and defiance on their own children, and this was evident from the playground to the lack of party invitations. My child had become off-limits—an outcast and a pariah.

After a rousing afternoon of his rendition of Superman flying off buildings (the tables in his first-grade classroom), his teacher was sympathetic. Maybe he needed more attention, or perhaps, she suggested, there were learning differences. I was given names of PhDs, therapists, testing facilities, and the first letter of many requesting I find another school.

He was diagnosed at almost seven years old with ADHD. At that time, we did what the doctors advised: Ritalin and Adderall, both amphetamines that killed his appetite and kept him awake all night. Reading the side effects of these medications years later and knowing what he went through, I could only pray for his forgiveness. His steady and progressive descent into a troubled psyche began the moment the drugs took over. There were endless visits to the doctor, blood tests to correct dosage levels, and medication changes that precipitated mood swings. There were bouts of depression and more schools that wouldn't accept him or soon dismissed him. This resulted in an endless spiral of despair that nipped at the weak spots, as socialization, educational productivity, and self-worth steadily became self-loathing. The drugs kept him awake at night, and the company of video games became insidious and constant.

When the suicide attempt failed, he was placed in a recovery center from eight to three for two weeks. At the end of that period, I was given another name, this time an educational consultanting firm in Palo Alto. The staff at the recovery center did not believe it was in Scooter's best interest to return to the environment that had created his despair—and this center counted as his fifth school in six years. The consulting firm sought to glean insight into the next step; interviews with Scooter, testing, and counseling. Where would he thrive and grow: military school, a therapeutic environment, or boot camp? There was a timing issue, as this eruption happened in the spring. It was too soon for most summer programs and too late to join an existing program. He wound up with early entrance to a summer wilderness program. A month later he was in Idaho, hiking, trekking, and talking to professionals. This was an interim program, and though I hoped he would "get better" and return in August to assume the duties of an eighth grader, the prospects were not encouraging.

Reg and I made the decision to put our trust in the hands of the experts. We knew we were in uncharted territory and we were forced to trust; the Palo Alto firm was consummate and we had to put our trust for his future in the hands of professionals. From the eight-week outdoor program, he was segued into a year-round program in middle-of-nowhere Montana, where he was to spend the next three years.

Above is the first note under the door that Scooter delivered to me, during a trial visit home from the Montana program. Before he was to leave for an evening out with friends, I requested a note, giving him the same freedoms Ashton had been afforded. It was a leap of faith on my part. He arrived home at the agreed-upon hour without mishap or misdeed. He did not let me down, and the rebuilding of our relationship began with this note. Had I realized what the positive long-term outcome of his four years away from home would be, I could have dismissed the guilt that would burden me for years. I believed I was an incapable parent who was to blame for all his problems.

In the late 1990s into the 2000s, Scooter's school, far away, was a respite from the troubled teens of the middle child. Remember when I said I thought I would drop my children off at expensive private schools and pick them up after their senior year, fit to go to any university in the world? And excel at the passion I had helped develop and nurture?

Another myth shattered.

I blamed myself for not being able to raise my child. My ex-husband, the father of my children, blamed me, too. The votes had been tallied and I was the loser.

Yet, through the diligence of their staff and the unabashed optimism of a mother and stepfather, Scooter's life was saved, collateral damage notwithstanding.

The hole in the family needed to heal. The other two needed space from the erratic behavior of their middle sibling. I needed to regain my self-esteem

Dear Tooth Fairy,
I dropped my tooth on the stair and when I find it I'll
put it under my pillow
Love
—Scooter

Precious, precious child, filled with possibility. The heartache that comes with unconditional love can be unbearable. Only the memory of innocence can sometimes ease the pain.

There is nothing like tradition and milestone moments

to bond each family member with strength and closeness. Tradition helps alienate confusion; you know the family you belong to by your shared memories, but many memories are best forgotten. Our special memories surrounded Christmas and Easter.

Thanksgiving was fun at one time, and J. R.'s favorite holiday, but then my mother ruined it by repeatedly taunting Cinnamon about her weight, which usually coincided with the serving of the pie. My mother didn't even drink, so there was no excuse except meanness. There were other milestones.

That first lost tooth was an event. Scooter placed his tooth inside the special heart-shaped tooth fairy pillow complete with buttoned pocket for the to-be-delivered treasure. As he was sliding headfirst down the banister, the tooth went flying. The resulting search by the adults finally produced the hidden gem just in time for the tooth fairy's arrival.

I knew I wanted two children. He was my second Clomid child, born as a result of so much effort. Even though I loved being an only child when I was young, I later realized how much better it would have been to share with a loving brother or sister—especially during the long, slow demise of my father due to dementia or the trials of my mother's stroke. There is no guarantee there would have been a loving bond with a sibling, but I still longed for something I didn't have.

With Scooter, it took only two years to get pregnant. The middle child was born with a vengeance due to the labor-inducing drug, Pitocin. This drug brings new meaning to heavy-metal labor. Since their father missed the birth of the first, I was determined not to go through the second one alone. The second baby was two weeks late and looked to be over nine pounds, so I made the choice for what the doctor called a "social induction." Had he been the first, he would have been the last.

I went into the hospital around ten in the morning, with plenty of time at home for a nice shower, hair, and makeup. I was just having a baby, after all. I'd done it before. This time had all the same prep as the first one and then an IV. By the time I asked—no, screamed—for an epidural, the delivering doctor leaned over my terrified face and calmly said, "It's too late." Interestingly, I wouldn't remember as much of this birth as I did the first one, which was a blessing. I remember a rush of care and concern when Ashton arrived to meet his little brother, and that overwhelming feeling for the firstborn rather than the newborn left me feeling guilty. It was too late to decide if I'd done the right thing by having another child, but my thoughts were with my firstborn and how he was going to react at no longer being the center of my entire attention. I had learned a lesson with the first, when I was home in less than twenty-four hours and tending to the everyday household chores. This time they had to pry me out of the hospital. I knew what was waiting for me at home, and I much preferred being waited on. Baby to the nursery, please!

Before I was even discharged from the hospital, off again went the father—a familiar pattern, though this time there was an in-house nanny to help. I returned to volunteering shortly after his birth, and life continued on with a familiarity I didn't mind.

Baby grew and certainly had his own personality that was very different from the first child. He wasn't content to be read to. He wanted to slide down the banister railing at eighteen months and charge headlong into anything that seemed likely to generate angst, panic, or general chaos in the family. He loved the attention of it all, and it was apparent from an early age that he was bonding with his father in a way Ashton never did. Little did I see the forecast predicting Scooter's terrifying feelings of abandonment. By the time he was two, the seeds of a double loss were sown and sprouting for the little boy and his mommy. I lost my live-in father-in-law that year and my touchstone of unconditional love. I was the one who wept inconsolably at his funeral, while John sat stoically, turned inward and cold. J. R. had always been there to read to Ashton, and he had been unceasingly patient with Scooter. Before he was wheeled into a surgery he would not live through, he told me he was sorry he couldn't help with Scooter that day. The boy's activity had been too much for him, and he just wasn't feeling up to the lively pace. An abdominal aneurism bled out in surgery, and there was no chance for me to tell him how vital a link to my sanity he had been.

I was seeing less and less of my husband and becoming more and more a fixture in small-town life: chairman of this, committee head of that. Women do that when their children begin school. It is a bond of young and not-so-young mothers that creates stability for families in a community. Parents have a desire for their children to excel in school, and many feel their focus on school-related activities will bolster their child's social and educational well-being. Not only are parents interested in academic success; we are obsessed with our children's social acceptance. It is as if we were in school all over again, remembering the taunts, bullying, and hurt we incurred at the hands of a wretchedly sociopathic eight-year-old school chum, and we vow to hover about so the same thing will not happen to our second coming of Christ.

Having a child who is labeled "different" by his teachers and administration at the preschool level guarantees you interesting times ahead. By the second year of preschool, our adorable hell on wheels was demonstrating his two-headed angel/demon personality to everyone he came into contact with. He was not mean, he simply pushed limits to the brink, and he was definitely the reason limits were created. The angelic side lay just under the surface of the need to whip the world into a frenzy and then sit back and watch the show.

When he discovered gaming at around age six, it provided him with a built-in reward system to gain confidence and satisfaction. By the time he was in fourth or fifth grade, he started connecting to other players in a way he couldn't connect to other children his age and in person.

Yo, Whazup??
I had a good time at work
Hope you had fun at the party.
Got a phone from the water!
Hope it works!
—Scooter

I became intrusive in my children's daily lives with constant corrections: grammar, etiquette, how to dress, and daily directives in list form that I didn't realize could serve to squash creativity and lead to feelings of little worth. My methods, which I considered helpful, could have signaled to them I thought nothing they did was good enough, yet at the time I thought I was teaching them the correct way, the perfectionist way, my right way. I couldn't imagine that I might have been over-parenting to make up for my lack of physical presence. If I had recognized that my air of superiority covered my insecurities and meant that finding fault replaced finding joy, I might have broken the pattern of rigid parenting that didn't allow for compassionate understanding and celebrating differences.

Scooter's tactile differences were evident in his constant search for the way things worked. He took apart radios, computers, toys, tools, kitchen appliances, stereo systems, and boom boxes. They would get put back together with a few parts to spare, and most of the time they continued to work. More than once I would scream in shock and pain in the middle of a dark night, having stepped on a missing screw or washer from his latest demolition.

His healthy curiosity regarding how things were made was unflagging, even in the face of my irritation and injured feet. Unfortunately, I viewed this as negative behavior. If I had realized the act was not destructive in nature but hands-on learning, my small irritations could have been turned into moments of accommodations to his learning patterns. Yet, I continued the attempt of squashing a square peg into a round hole.

(spelling and punctuation left as written)

Dear Mom,
I'm very very, very, very sorry. I love you a lot. I'm so so, so sorry about Tuesday night. Do you forgive me? I hope so. I'm so greatful to you. Without our caring my life would be miserable. With out you I woudent have a school, a place to stay, or a life. I feel so bad. If you didn't care I would be on the streets.

Whith out you I woulden't have super Nintendo,
Sega Gensis, gym, a car, toys chess, Sandy, acting ballet,
sometime soccer, tee ball, and friends.
Love
Scooter

Some interesting foreshadowing here. He would lose everything and wind up living on the streets by age twenty-three. It happened. Gaming issues, they happened. Sandy, the first of dozens of therapists, happened. Friends, not so much.

I was the one yet to be diagnosed with EOD: early onset delusion.

1) I thought he needed to be fixed.
2) I thought I could fix him.

Neither could have been further from the truth.

I was conflicted, believing the educational system should be equipped to educate children who displayed differences. My hair-trigger excuses for his behavior stemmed from my desire to protect him from being hurt. It was hard for me to shut that defense mechanism down and always would be. He'd finally get to a point where he didn't need it anymore. He'd win his hard-fought battle, but it would take twenty-six years.

If you are lucky and you learn to keep your mouth shut, one day your kids will talk to you because they want to, not because they must. I have found this to be one of the most rewarding things about having children. But it only happens if you are lucky.

It would take time, but eventually he would solicit my advice about how to break up with someone he had once loved and probably still did. How hard is that to articulate, to know, when you are under thirty? Hell, it's hard to know no matter how old you are. To ask for guidance at a pivotal moment put some pressure on me to come up with the answer that would not be interfering yet would hopefully help. Time for a deep breath, for a quick prayer, and to say what you think. "Don't be long. Tell the truth. Accept the tears. Quick is less painful. No, you cannot be friends."

And lo and behold, he took my advice. He actually called me, and the first thing I asked was, "Did you sleep with her first?" To his credit, the answer was negative, even though he said he had thought about it. His friends had encouraged him to have sex first and then break up. In a most heartfelt moment, I told him how proud I was of his decision, even if he had wrestled with the penis devil. Common decency had prevailed.

How was I to imagine this from the child who had broken my heart repeatedly? My relationship with him can be encapsulated by a quote from Fredrick Douglas: "It is easier to build strong children than to repair broken men."

Douglas, born in 1818, was an African American social reformer, abolitionist, orator, writer, and statesman, and he sired three boys and two girls who were activists their entire life. He did a better job at parenting than I. It's a good day when two of the three are not in some type of distress.

Had fun
Got pulled over.
Pat yelling out the car window.
Small town blues.
—Scooter

Raising children as a single woman in a small coastal California town in the 1990s had its perks. I had rented out the family home in the hopeless dream that I would be able to move back into it once my business was going strong. Little did I realize it would take years to turn enough of a profit in my new business to afford that kind of space. Even as I sold my beloved rings, bracelets, earrings, and necklaces to pay the rent and the mortgage, I believed there was a chance to have our old life back. That all ended with the eventual sale of the dream house two years later.

I lived, with all three kids, in one of a group of identical one-bedroom apartments, stacked on top of each other, that totaled eight hundred square feet. We lived here for four years behind the business I slaved 24/7 to get off the ground. It took that small village of friends, neighbors, and the police department to keep me apprised of my children's actions until I decided dating a sugar daddy might have its rewards. During the six months I attempted to be happy with this kind man, I had a nanny who stayed with the children after school until I came home from work at nine. She worked for me and was an anchor during the growth of my business, both for the children and for me. The sugar daddy lasted 180 days. Katherine lasted four years.

Hey, had fun
Thanx for letting me go out.
—Scooter

The years he spent in Idaho and Montana were fraught with great happiness, intense grief, frustrated feelings of failure, and continued worry and prayer. And that was just me!

He did well after a while, but not at first. The adjustment was difficult for him, although so much easier for the family left behind. His erratic behavior, caused by the prescription drugs and clinical depression, was unnatural to live with. Another round of guilt threatened to undo me soon after he left the family home. A peace settled upon the remaining family as the daily angst, yelling, fists through the walls, and other regular horrors were over. I think we all suffered from post-traumatic stress. I felt both damned and guilty for being glad he was gone.

I had been living the life of a person with multiple-personality disorder; I was one way at home and another at work. The happy face was left at the door in the umbrella stand to don and discard as necessary—a one-dimensional reality. That trait became a keen survival technique and would serve me well for years to come.

For him, the prospect of what had been promised (or threatened) became a reality. Though I don't pretend to know what was going through his mind at the beginning of that summer, I do know he attempted a few phone pleas for forgiveness.

When he arrived in Montana, he lived in a tent on the property and had to "earn" his way into the house. As time progressed, he became accustomed to the drill—homework completed on time, chores done, therapy in groups and privately—so, his place in the main house was assured. He shared the Montana program school experience with eight other young people in various stages of recovery.

We were able to visit at Thanksgiving, after he had been there for six months. But I hadn't seen him in nine months. Reg went with Scooter on a hundred-mile kayaking trip on a nearby river for fathers and boys. I wouldn't have lived through an outdoor camping experience, especially one of those hardcore trips where you pack out whatever you bring in, including a portable toilet. My mind didn't understand this concept. I support no plastic bags, recycling glass (wine) bottles, and eating leftovers—but really, bears shit in the woods, right? What on earth is the reasoning behind dragging the proceeds of the morning constitutional out of the woods?

We stayed at a lovely bed-and-breakfast close by that Thanksgiving. Scooter was allowed an overnight, and it was the first time he had been with his siblings in quite a while. While I walked a fine line of behavioral assessment, Scooter's brother and sister picked up where they had left off—loud, raucous, and loving. When we were all together, the kids and adults attempted to be a family just like the quaint Cleavers, playing Monopoly after dinner, soaking in the hot tub (OK, a California Cleaver family), and taking hikes in the Montana wilderness. Of course, the Cleavers didn't have daily sessions with psychologists in the mix, but I'm sure June, a happy homemaker mother, needed a good shrink. After all, she lived in a perfect suburban family with an all-knowing husband, a wise older son, and a goofy yet kindhearted younger son. It's the stuff Zoloft was made for.

The second time we visited, we stayed at a real motel in the small Montana town close to the school. Motels have a certain air about them, and this worn-out, street-front, mid-century classic had seen better days. While I was finicky about bathrooms and bed sheets, overlooking the décor was second to the morning breakfast offering of fruit and toast. The faded maraschino cherry atop pale green canned grapes was simply not what this Californian recognized as fruit. This was as close to camping as I wanted to get, yet there was a time I romanticized a grand scheme involving renting an RV, and loading up the kids, cat, and dog for a summer outing across the United States to see the national parks. The fantasy included the traveling band of opposites all agreeing on what to see next, when to dine, and how many miles to travel in a day. The RV would have had plenty of space, including a bathroom or two, and be free of the smell of Febreze that wafted through the Montana motel room.

The RV would not have had a noisy, ancient, under-the-window air conditioner/heater that spewed toxic air or be parked adjacent to a streetlight that ever so slightly interfered with a peaceful night's rest. I'm glad I can say that RV trip never happened, as we are still alive and have a modicum of sanity that would have been demolished had my great summer adventure ever come to fruition.

Although Scooter continued to be medicated while he was away, the constant one-on-one attention and daily therapy helped him. It gave him insight, understanding, and the ability to see his truth. We as a family had to face our truths as well, and that wasn't always a pretty picture.

At some point John decided to take a trip one weekend to visit. The stepmother arrived in middle-of-nowhere Montana in a full-length mink coat, disdainfully sniffed around, and asked to be taken back to the hotel. They left within forty-eight hours.

Scooter was surprised and genuinely glad to see them, yet by this time his father was terminally ill. The brittle cold of a Montana winter sent him and his wife scurrying back to the warmth of the hotel room and shortly back on a plane for California's mild winter temperatures. Scooter was left with the memory of only a couple shared meals with his father and stepmother during their short time together. He was happy that his father had taken the time and effort to make sure he was OK, which was the entire purpose for the trip. I imagined his father was looking for a way to undermine my decision to send him there, yet he left Montana without a scene.

⁓

I'm home safe, obviously
Thanks for the fun birthday.
I enjoyed today (err, yesterday)
Thanks for letting me borrow
the car. It only has
some minor damage from the 7-car pileup, but no
worries . . . Just playing
Love,
Scooter
(You thought there was a pileup, just for a minute didn't you?)

He was only one who didn't have car issues. He built a car while living in San Diego. He was so proud of his work! The car was stolen and probably ended up in Tijuana in a parts shop.

There was no insurance on the car. Lesson #43: You love it and you can't afford to replace it? You'd better insure it. I seemed to get a statement in the mail daily from either the life, health, long-term care, home, or auto insurance company. But, how do you buy insurance on a child?

And I'm not talking about insurance on their life. I'm talking about insuring that the love of your life will be safe, not get sick or be in pain, not end up hurt or homeless. Most would say a good education is a great place to start. There are many ways to become educated. Unfortunately, one of the most popular routes is known as the "hard way." This term has interesting implications for young people, and prophetic resonance for those of us over thirty. The hard way usually refers to life lessons created by trial and error as opposed to learning in schools or, better yet, from the parents who adore you and probably learned the hard way themselves, long before you were a glimmer in their eye.

Scooter also lived in his car on the streets in San Diego. I didn't know about that until it was long over. As it turns out, I didn't know quite a bit until it was over. He said it was only a few months; a few hours would have been a ghastly reality for me to comprehend.

My Catholic guilt reared its ugly head again, strongly, when I discovered Scooter was living in his car, yet I reasoned with my demons. I supposed, to find his way out, he needed the experience of living without toilet, toothbrush, or the ability to be tucked in. He would do it his way, not the way I wanted it to be. Yet, learning the hard way has its advantages. One has a tendency not to forget the lesson very easily.

One day, he came to us at around age twenty-three or twenty-four and said he didn't want to continue his education. He was only doing it for us, and oh, by the way, he wasn't really going to classes anyway. I had been pressuring him to stay in school by keeping him funded. If he stopped going, it meant we'd stop paying for school, food, car, phone, and insurance . . . everything. He knew the rules: as long as you are in school, the bank remains open; once school is out, the bank is closed. Now he wanted the bank to close and, moreover, he was demanding to hand back the keys to the bank, so we knew he meant business.

I'd enabled him for years until I finally forced him to say, "I'm not going to school. I am only doing this because you want me to, not because I want to. So cut me off, let me be, leave me alone, I love you."

So that is what we did. Reluctantly for me, easier for the stepfather, the money stopped. Scooter quit the school he wasn't attending, and the downhill slope became more slippery. We did continue to pay for his cell phone and health insurance. He got work with an IT company answering phones and solving folks' computer issues. He had funny stories, but he really wasn't going anywhere.

He shared the story about a distraught woman who phoned him to say she had spilled her latte in the cup holder of her computer.

"Cup holder?" our courteous young man inquired.

"Yes, you know, the cup holder. You push it in on the side and it pops out."

"Oh yes, that," he answered. "That actually isn't a cup holder."

She was shocked into silence.

"It's for a disc or DVD," he told the amazed woman. "And I'm afraid your latte has probably done some damage that I can't help you with over the phone. I suggest you take it into your local computer store and see if there is anything they can do to help!"

He was hilarious in his delivery of this story. He probably could have been a great stand-up comedian or a psychologist. Yet, he was looking for his passion, and it didn't include IT or giving emotional advice to strangers. For him, luckily, the best was yet to come—and I am a living testament to the fact I didn't murder him, though the thought crossed my mind on numerous occasions.

Work was good
but time for
much needed
sleep!
—Scooter
p.s. Thanks for the Mers ☺

Mers are meringues, a Trader Joe's special. His favorite!

This was from the child who from age six through eleven would eat five sugar packets at a time. When he recognized a twenty-ounce serving of Mountain Dew contained the same amount of sugar, he started wolfing the soft drink. Drinking the soda was more acceptable than straight-up sugar packets. He had recently graduated to the meringues, an even more socially acceptable sugar rush than sodas.

In the years between the end of high school, which included a year at a Chinese university outside of Beijing, and the work world, Scooter tried several jobs designed to buy enough ramen noodles to offset starvation. Ramen didn't have anything to do with the Asian educational year; it was just the cheapest thing to eat.

One job was at an IT call center. As a boomer, I too needed a call center or personal assistant for my computer issues. Since I had the inside extension number, I called frequently. Scooter would answer and scold me, saying, "Google is your best friend," implying that I should be researching the answer myself instead of asking for help. He implied that I might learn something I would remember if I did it myself instead of someone doing it for me. His idea had merit, yet I figured I was old enough to be allowed all the help I could muster. I was unwilling to risk the

124 Notes After Midnight

time it would take to study the computer lexicon that might help solve a simple problem. I regarded this task like a foray into a foreign landscape, and I wanted a seasoned tour guide.

On one afternoon phone call, he listened quietly, assessing my grave situation. "I know exactly what the problem is," he said. "Please get a pen and paper. Now write this down. The letters ID, the number 10, the letter T."

I looked down at the paper: IDIOT.

He laughed; I didn't.

After that, I took his advice and Googled first.

Scooter did have an instinctual grasp of computers. He was engaged and alert, interested and focused. He took them apart and put them together, much like the Lego days, except now he was receiving a paycheck for that talent. In the classroom, from first to fourth grade, he was bored and acted out. Parents in this "me, me, me" generation claim boredom as a sign of genius and not enough stimulation in a standardized school experience. Having taught hundreds of children by the time I gave birth to my three, I knew genius level was rare. Everything from technology to a dopamine deficiency had been blamed for boredom and the inability to pay attention. Either way, there seemed to be an entire generation of children being raised by Baby Einstein believers, paralleling the advent of the age of Nintendo and the constant stream of information available at our fingertips, and creating, at least in their parents' mind, the child who would cure the world's ills. I held no such fantasies about Scooter.

Scooter was self-taught with the world at his computer fingertips, and, as the traditional method of learning (rote memorization) repelled his desire to learn in school, he learned at his own speed and only what he wanted to study. Regurgitating facts didn't challenge his curiosity. There was one year and one teacher in his elementary education who became a pivotal inspiration: Mr. Patrick, in fifth grade. I knew when I walked into that classroom that the match was made in heaven. The room was filled with learning stations overflowing with objects to promote inquisitive questionings. Airplane models hanging haphazardly from the ceiling, random book stacks were throughout the room, and desks were piled with papers and journals. Both teacher and pupil were learning challenged, and it proved to be a year of growth Scooter hadn't experienced.

By the last year of elementary education, Scooter had been in four different schools, from Montessori to alternative educational days. The alternative was a three-day-a-week, half-day classroom that taught knitting and decoupage. My wish list contained a line requesting a hand-knit beanie, yet the three-day week was too challenging for a single mother. Scooter had no objection to the lack of formality, but it only lasted three months before we were on to the next possibility. What we found for that one wonderful fifth grade year was the amalgamation of independent thinking and core subjects.

The baby boomers' children are a different breed from those raised by Depression Era or Golden Age (1950s) parents. Scooter, Ashton, and Cinnamon watched me struggle though a recession that began in California in the late 1980s and became a pivotal reason for my divorce. The impact was implicit; it was difficult to fulfill adult responsibilities especially after the great recession of 2008 created job loss and student debt. Ashton came home from university for the summers only, and Scooter moved back in for a while after he went from one job to another, searching for a passion to follow. He simply couldn't make enough money to get by, even on a steady diet of ramen noodles. He had replaced the steady flow of Mountain Dew with Jack and Coke, which didn't add clarity to his dismal outlook. The sugar packets of his yesterday looked quite benign compared to the options he would choose while attempting to find himself.

~~~

Sokay. I'll be up!
Love
—Scooter

He woke up at twenty-six, at rock bottom and living in his car on a diet of uncooked Top Ramen. He was registered for the spring session at a local community college but decided he wasn't going to attend. On the first day of school, when he should have been in class, he drove aimlessly around the outskirts of the campus reflecting on his decision. Two attractive girls were anxiously hitchhiking towards the campus, and he picked them up. They chatted with Scooter and thanked him for his help, as they didn't want to be late for class. The brief conversation included questions about his school classes, potential major, and a life goal. The short ride was filled with burning questions and made-up answers.

His bullshit lines were enough to keep them engaged during the drive, and it was his turning point. He tells the story of being so embarrassed at having to lie that he knew he needed to change his life. Pulling his car to the side of the road, he vowed to make something of his life. He didn't know how at that moment, but he knew something drastically had to happen.

Months later, his decision to enter the military was not a choice I supported. The plan had been hatched between

Scooter and Reg, who was "once a marine, always a marine." The conversation with me about this life choice was clearly a well-thought-out campaign to win me over. No marine, no army, no front-line tactical weapon combat, yet the decision of Special Ops navy diver would be fraught with intense underwater training, physical reformation of a couch potato physique, and a mindset I wasn't sure he could achieve. My horror and abject terror of open water would now be a long-range life reality. My fear of drowning, witnessed by the two seat belt cutters and window smasher tools I kept in every car I ever drove, would be in my dreams and nightmares for my second-born now for the rest of my life. He did have a direction, though, and when I allowed myself to stop thinking about drowning, I was grateful that he'd found a calling and that living in his car would be a thing of the past.

Hey,
I'm back, the gym was
good, Pat might join us at
work tomorrow.
—Scooter

Working out was better than hitting the brewskies! Depression that leads to addiction comes in many forms. Later he would drink too much to ease the pain. He was lost, and I couldn't do one thing to help him find himself.

He had to create his future, and since Reg was a former marine, Scooter envisioned with Reg this future for himself many times but unbeknownst to me. Scooter wanted to enter the military, and both my son and my husband knew the entire idea was not going to "play well in Peoria"—another of Mother's sayings that means something's not going to go over well on Main Street America, meaning me.

Given that I belong to the "mother" demographic, frontline military engagement for Scooter was out of the question. "No marines—your mother will kill me," was a direct quote from Reg. Scooter came from a long line of navy men. My father, his biological father, his stepbrother—all navy.

He came up with a terrific plan, though at the time I cried and wailed and gnashed my teeth (all for naught). The stubborn gene that all my children have as a dominant trait came from me. Obstinacy would get me far in life. Think about those poor folks who never can decide. We all know them. Indecision stems from anxiety. We fear making the wrong decision and suffering consequences, or we worry about making a mistake and feeling guilty, remiss, exposed, or ignorant. Sometimes we are paralyzed by a fear of hurting or alienating another.

This is a variation on countless conversations I've heard couples having:

"Where would you like to go today on our day off, the beach or the mountains?"

"Well, I don't know, where would you like to go?"

"The beach is nice this time of year, and I enjoy the fresh air of the mountains, too. What do you think?"

By the time they've decided to forget both the beach and the mountains, the mayo in the potato salad has developed botulism from sitting out in the sun too long. Now, that is a real problem. Mother used to say, "Decide, even if it is wrong." I would have said I wanted to go to the beach and been done with it.

Navy won. After researching potential jobs, Special Operations diver bubbled to the top. Aside from a parachute specialist, that would have been my *last* choice. It was right up there with nuclear waste management and demolition. The navy offered a signing bonus for nuclear. Really, who would sign up for that? Not enough tea in Three Mile Island for me.

Becoming a navy diver requires a physically fit specimen with expanded lung capacity and the strength of a brute work animal. At the time of this monumental decision, getting off the sofa and away from the gaming console for Scooter was an effort. I wondered if it could happen.

Scooter began a rigorous diet, gave up the Jack and Coke (we share that passion), and dropped twenty while dropping twenty—pushups, that is. In six months, he was a hunk. Beyond the physical changes, his mental outlook driven by raw ambition to succeed was exhilarating. He was becoming his own man with a drive I hadn't seen.

I watched the young people in the YouTube videos carrying cement blocks the entire length of a swimming pool without surfacing for breath. The only positive note in the video was that it was filmed in an indoor pool. As everyone knows, the ocean is filled with sharks just waiting to take a leg off or creatures on the sandy bottom waiting to bite your toes. The pool worked for me, but the idea of lugging bricks not so much.

That was only this tip of the training iceberg. He had pounds to lose—and not just ten pounds either. This professional couch potato had over thirty pounds to drop in a short period of time.

He was going to have to build stamina and lay off the booze, weed, cookies, and candy. I felt confident this didn't have a hoot in hell of coming to fruition.

I couldn't have been more wrong. He created his own success by a six-step process:

1) He decided what he wanted.
2) He found out what it would take to get to the finish line (i.e., education).
3) He kept the goal in sight.
4) He allowed for brief deviations.
5) He understood, even though he was twenty-six years old and getting a late start, that it's never too late to start.
6) He internalized the idea that if you don't start, you will never finish.

Before I knew it, he was off to boot camp near Lake Michigan. In six weeks, the guy who left without a backwards glance was in the navy now.

Flying into O'Hare for his graduation from boot camp was a reflective time. Once again, history repeats itself—or does it? It wasn't his history; it was mine that I was confronting. I hadn't seen him for weeks, just like when he was in Montana. But this reunion was to celebrate that he had achieved a huge goal that he had set. Success with a capital S.

The theory of historical repeating is based on the idea that we cannot learn from a mistake until we experience the mistake. That seems fine for the first go around, but here I was again facing the same set of circumstances, different army. It would take more than that present moment to truly understand why things kept repeating themselves. Was it about control, fearing the loss of love, or never being sure control was there in the first place? And, how much of it was about me? Clearly, he had his own demons to deconstruct. Often, there is more than one actor on stage or in the wings during any production. Our family was no different. Dismantling years of guilt is a daunting prospect.

Our instinctual and familial early relationships create the patterns for adult—or some clearly non-adult—behavior as we face issues that can be trying at best and horrific at worst.

The field of neuroscience is exploding with findings about how the brain works, much of which backs up the notion that significant relationships and experiences in our lives can imprint unconscious memories in our brains—memories that can be triggered later in life and lead to certain feelings and behaviors without us even realizing it. These patterns, if recognized, with time become new learned behavior. Most of us operate on child-hood relationships, good or bad, which shape our ability to trust, find personal security, and become independent.

Basically, Scooter and I share an optimistic outlook, which is interesting in the face of his youthful misdeeds. I found the camaraderie of his boot camp group of paramount importance to him. Another recruit came out to a meal with us. For me, the more the merrier; for my son, those around you are family—and he'd already learned that, in times of war, you count on them as they count on you.

I thought about my father, who would pick up every kid walking on the way to grade school until his car had kids coming out the windows. It was a light blue VW bug, and it looked like a Toontown clown car by the time we arrived at the elementary school. Though he was the height of embarrassment to me then, I'd remember him for his patience and generosity.

It would be interesting be the fly on the wall while my three kids talk about me after my death and what phobias, stories of neglect, and unhealthy relationships are due to their parents' obvious shortcomings. I only hope they'll be forgiving.

Had fun
Got pulled over.
Pat yelling out the car window.
Small town blues.
—Scooter

Raising very different children produced a completely different set of circumstances and public interactions. I would get a phone call about Scooter skateboarding down the middle of the street without a helmet from the friendly neighborhood police department when he was younger and, later on, a "how ya doin'" from one of his buddies on the police force. These special men and women, with not an appreciable amount to do in small-town USA, were there to protect my children. Many times, I believe they protected them from my wrath. My children would remember me saying many times, "If you are still alive, I plan to kill you!"

The medical community was less supportive.

I continued to believe the doctors knew what they were talking about, and I was desperate for relief—relief for me, relief for Scooter, relief for our family. I believed doctors were there to bring us hope, and I believed in the power of prescription.

The vast majority of prescriptions for amphetamine and

methylphenidate are for children diagnosed with ADHD. Known by the popular name of Ritalin, this drug has been used to treat ADHD for over fifty years. For a parent, the decision to medicate is huge, and it weighed on my mind then and later.

Scooter was a statistic. Diagnosed at six years old, Ritalin was the first line of defense, prescribed to help the teachers in his private school deal with his over-the-top behavior. His first-grade teacher really tried, unlike others. His problem or gift was that he was a totally likeable child. He was bright and always had a ready smile. Even when getting a normal set of vaccines at three years old, he never cried. He simply looked at the doctor after she gave him the injection and said, "You hurt me." She started to cry as she apologized.

Some of his behaviors seem somewhat humorous in retrospect—like the time he climbed a light pole in front of our condo and threatened to leap off headfirst. I don't remember how I got him down. Another time he was angry and said he was going to hold his breath until he died. Well, had I been thinking, I would have known he would just pass out and that would be that. But no, Mighty Mom came to the rescue. I pushed, pulled, tugged, pried, and wormed my way into his deadlock grip around his neck. When he finally released his breath, he was mad enough to put me up against the wall by my neck.

I called the hospital and asked what to do. Their simplistic suggestion was, "Well, put him in the car and bring him up, and we'll check on him." By this time he was as tall as I was and outweighed me by forty pounds. I was supposed to invite him into the car for a trip to get fitted for a straitjacket? This made no sense to me whatsoever. Yet, I don't give up easily. I somehow got him in the car and off we went for an afternoon hospital visit.

The attending psychiatrist took one look at his neck and back marks, which were beginning to welt in the shape of hand and fingerprints, and pronounced me guilty of child abuse.

This was the second time I'd been accused of this.

Maybe the world was seeing the real me, and I was just hiding under this cloak of regularity and conformity. Maybe I was incapable of raising children alone. Maybe "everyone," whoever they were, was right. I was a failure at motherhood.

But no, I had not abused him. I was attempting to save his life. Fortunately, I had the backing of our family pediatrician who vouched for my decency, and I was able to leave the hospital with new medication for my son. Throughout the years searching for his "cure," it's a wonder no one ever offered *me* drugs.

Scooter's envelope-pushing personality was exhausting.

His penchant for the Spider-Man/Batman complex was harrowing to me and the rest of the family. On his first vacation trip to England at eight, his understanding of "Mind the gap"— the area where you're not supposed to stand between the safety of the platform and the speeding underground train—meant, "See how close you get to the edge of the train platform, with a train arriving, so Mommy can start to scream!" And then he would offer an angelic smile and say, "What?" He had a thing about trains that followed well into adulthood.

It didn't help to know that Aldgate Station, on the Circle and Metropolitan Lines in central London, is built on a massive plague pit, where more than one hundred bodies are buried. It was clear to me, from my son's behavior, that he would soon be added to the pit. He simply never listened to my reasoning—and that was a trend that continued all the way up to his enrollment in the US Navy.

From five years old to eighteen, he made the rounds of psychologists, psychiatrists, family therapists, medical doctors, and all manner of well-meaning counselors, mood changers, and mind benders. He took Ritalin, Adderall, and Dexedrine. By the time he finally said, "Enough, I will not take any more drugs," it was a wonder we weren't all dead from his constant need for attention and thrill-seeking.

Good Morning Mummy
Alex and I say
Thank you for dinner.
—Love Scooter

Mummy? Since when did the entire family become so British?

This was a family dinner night. We had these dinners regularly, and the three tried in vain not to be available. There is something quite bucolic about the fantasy of everyone sitting down to a beautifully cooked dinner, shoes on, hair combed, teeth brushed, matching socks (OK, there goes the OCD), a great attitude about the day, and a readiness to share it. I am not sure what they pay the actors in those photos to sit still and smile, but just once I would have liked to have that scene play in my dining room with my family. I simply couldn't pay them enough to show up.

So I came up with theme nights, a great concept for a fun evening. The most memorable was Hawaiian night.

I decorated the entire first floor in fishing net, and the stairs were festooned to look like a deep-sea ahi (tuna) hunt aboard a seaworthy fishing vessel. The dining room décor featured coconuts, leis, and fake flowers. The children were forbidden to come downstairs during the pre-event decoration, and I made a real Hawaiian dinner: poi, poke, and white rice served by Mom in a coconut shell bra and grass skirt. (Yes, I really went the extra mile.) I had to make teriyaki chicken to appease the meat-eaters at the table. Everyone was happy! Right!?

Years later, they would remember that night with horror and tell sordid tales of lasting PDS—Post Dramatic Stress. At least it would give us something to talk about when we all sat at the table together and remembered the old days.

Yo Yo Yo, I got a train in my house . . .
10:15 home. . . .
Sorry late
—Scooter

Dope, Yo, Fly, My Bad, Chillin', Diss, Boo Ya!, Trippin', Aiiiright, Whatever!, Da Bomb, and Yadda Yadda Yadda—great slang from the 1990s. Scooter could use them all in one sentence.

Some of these terms would last, others would later be embarrassing. "Whatever" was always accompanied with a perfected eyeball roll.

Yadda, Yadda, Yadda, not one that would last beyond the '90s, was stolen from the iconic television program *Seinfeld* on the 153rd episode. But neither Seinfeld nor his writers invented the term. It can be traced to the controversial, countercultural comedian Lenny Bruce in the early 1960s. Bruce became a legend, not only for his dark ability to make people laugh, but for his use of on-stage obscenities that lead to a landmark decision in favor of freedom of speech.

Scooter had an ability to make others laugh. Did it come from the dark side, the way humor can mask depression and be a coping mechanism, an escape from daily problems? Scooter used slang and obscenity in the same way, regardless of who was in the room. The vulgarities seemed less about the shock value than his objective teaching tool. He believed that a word was simply that, a word. The meaning was made good or bad by the people listening. For a while, it became his mission to legitimize the entire vocabulary of curse words.

His use of colloquialisms was mild in comparison. "My bad" is like saying, "I recognize something happened that isn't good and that I had a part in it, but I'm not going to apologize because a) I don't feel like it, b) it won't change anything, or c) I really don't give a shit."

"Boo-ya" is kind of fun and came home with him after his China excursion. It means something awesome has just occurred, and it probably made the Boo-yaer's life more fulfilling. During the '80s and '90s, Boo-ya was urban slang for the sound of a shotgun being fired and, due to the popularity of gang culture in urban areas, the shotgun imitation sound was embraced and often used to the point where it came to mean other things, such as "Hell, yes!" "Right on!" "In yer face!" or simply "Yeaahh!"

It's ironic that the typical family unit is designed to create care, love, concern, and positive socialization. In turn, the very youth we revere are espousing the tenets of a perverse and dangerous unit of society. They dress like gangsters, drive cars like gangsters, and speak the lingo of the hood. Though a vast percentage of youth do not engage in illegal behavior associated with urban gangs, disengagement in middle class families leads to acceptance of behavior that was once unacceptable. Had I known the vulgarity was nothing compared to the suicide road, I would have stopped my infernal need for behavior correction and grammatical accuracy. Baggie pants and a poor vocabulary were less of a challenge than acute depression resulting in a suicide attempt.

Thanks for letting me stay at Pat's. It was fun!
Hope you had a good night sleep.
Love
—Scooter

As a youngster, Scooter's behavior was erratic, tempestuous, and sometimes wild. Parents wouldn't invite him to their child's birthday parties or "play dates." Whoever thought up that grim term? If there is any phrase that makes my eyeballs roll and gives me a pre-vomit feeling, that is it: an Americanism thought up by helicopter parents with too much time on their hands. Give the kids a bat and ball, kick them out the front door, and lock it behind them until dinner. May the strong survive!

There is, in every family, a lore—a retelling of past events that are shared on occasion as training tools for those with weak memories. These tales bear repetition to validate previous edicts and stringently remind all parties of the evils cast upon the family as temptation so stronger constitutions would prevail. The fallout from bad decisions were set aside for other, weaker families. Sounds very prophetic and almost biblical, you might be thinking, but I have never been profound, prophetic, or religious. For me, these moments came in children's events gone terribly wrong.

One story surrounds a five-year-old's birthday party. The guests at this party were the children of the wealthy, the anointed, and thus deemed to be the potential leaders of tomorrow—and they were only in kindergarten. Their parents were the movers of Silicon Valley and the shakers of the Bay Area; the birthday girl's family home on the eighteenth green with a million-dollar view, hot and cold running help, caterers, event planners, and a cast of hundreds to make sure it was all perfectly executed.

So there I was, a divorced mother of three, barely making ends meet, arriving with my brood. My boy runs to join the others, and I stand, somewhat awkwardly, watching the children play. Then the procession begins. Leprechauns leading the group representing St. Patrick's Day were in the parade. It was June. Something set my first nerve on edge. Following the chocolate gold coins came the life-sized Easter Bunny, replete with baskets for all the children and a full-blown Easter egg hunt. Lest we hungered for more visual stimulation, Santa arrived with twelve elves in a golf cart. The second, third, and fourth cart were filled with gifts for the anointed child and her court.

It was around that time that I looked at my son and said, "We're leaving." I thought he was going to have the meltdown of the century. "Leave? Are you kidding, this is the best party I've ever been to in my whole life!" As I dragged him to the car, I attempted to explain that the conscious choice of parents who give a five-year-old child the twelve days of Christmas, for real, was giving me palpitations. He clearly did not share my objection to the excess.

Once he was in his teens and wanted to have sleepovers, how could I say no? Plus, the Pat in Scooter's note and his family were very normal—and the kind of people I wanted Scooter to hang out with.

❧

Hey, I'm home
Work was good
but tough
Very tired
Must sleep
Zzzzzzzzz

As a child, Scooter never slept—he passed out. I would hear him playing in the living room or outside, and then nothing. It was only then I ran, quietly searching for the spot. He would have fallen on the ground or behind the sofa, fast asleep. He was a night owl from the beginning. His days and nights never got unmixed up. I was in my thirties, yet I was exhausted all the time chasing him around, living in a reversed world. Remember when moms say they've never been more fit than while caring for a toddler? Well, I looked like I had been working out at the gym a couple of hours a day on a stringent diet of lettuce leaves and shredded carrots.

Had he been the first child, there wouldn't have been three. I couldn't have physically managed it.

When children are two and three years old, they are quite busy, and Scooter was no exception. If there was ever a case for leashing a child, he was the one. When I was shopping at Macy's, he would be under the clothing racks at Mervyn's next door—laughing, always laughing at me while I made myself hoarse calling his name over and over. His gleeful laughter would give him away. When standing on a street corner waiting for a light to change, he would have his feet hanging over the edge of the

curb and leaning out as if to say, *I'm Superman, you can't get me!*
I do think he believed he had super powers.

My mother told me I had been on a leash as a child. She
always claimed it was easy to predict my whereabouts if I slipped
free. Most usually, I would be found in the department store's
sparkling jewelry case, attempting to try on a bracelet or other
shiny object. Some things don't change.

Unbelievably, Scooter only had one or two trips to the ER
for injuries. The first was at two and a half. He was supposed
to be enjoying Bible stories while I nodded off in a church pew
on a beautiful Sunday morning (I apparently needed my sleep
wherever I might catch it), but instead he decided to run the
fifty-yard dash down the rectory hallway. Full speed ahead for a
determined two-year-old can be fairly intense, especially when
meeting an object at rest, like the edge of an open door. I think
he could be heard wailing in the next county. The boy certainly
had a pair of lungs. The pastor's wife, the nursery angel, so loved
him; everyone loved him. And she was so upset that he had hurt
himself on her watch. But that was one of the few times he was
hurt enough to require medical attention.

He was nine and in France the next time. His brash and
headstrong personality, fueled by my ignorance, landed him in a
French hospital in the middle of the night. A carnival had come
to a nearby town in northern France where we were engaged in
the first of many house exchanges. I had traveled all my young
life with my parents and wanted to give my children the same
experiences. I had traveled the length and breadth of the United
States, so why not attempt the same feat in Europe? Northern
France on a dairy farm sounded like the perfect one-month vacation. My children should have the opportunity to see what farm

life is like. Shouldn't everyone? Up early in the morning, milk the cows, and smell the fresh-mown hay. Then, I could have cocktails at sunset. So off we went to the home of the vice mayor of this postage-stamp-sized berg as they winged their way to sunny—or in this case, foggy—coastal California.

We arrived, dazed, at the Paris airport and got directly into the rental car. Cars are notably smaller in Europe than we are used to here in the States. My family was driving a car the size of a carry-on rolling suitcase, without room for accessories or shoes. I sat in the middle, on the hump between two tired and argumentative children, while Reg drove and our eldest son navigated.

As usual, I had not bothered to map out our final destination. I mean, how big could France be, after all? It would be the longest day of my life. Our final stop was Brittany, as far as you can get before you fall into the Atlantic Ocean. We had arrived on a Monday, and everything was closed. We had three starving children and two adults in desperate need of alcohol. It was dinnertime and there was no dinner.

We knocked on a neighbor's door and attempted to tell our story. This was 1997, with no cell phones, apps, or translation capabilities. Somehow we were understood, and they pointed us to a small convenience store that was open. It was music to our ears until we went to pay and realized we had no francs, and the bank was closed.

We hadn't known we were exchanging houses with the mayor of this now-delightful village until the grocery store owners asked us where we were staying—and decided we would be good for the tab until the next day. Home we went with provisions and wine.

We were scheduled to stay for three weeks. On the first weekend we were there, the circus came to town. Actually it was next town over, and it was a traveling carnival, but why split hairs? We were off like the wind. There was cotton candy, a Ferris wheel, and bumper cars. It was my naiveté that fostered the belief that amusement parks around the world were policed for safety as in the United States. I had grown up in an amusement park until I was ten years old. This is not a statement about familial dysfunction, but an honest reality.

Below the bluffs of downtown St. Joseph, Michigan, hugging both the Lake Michigan shoreline and the St. Joseph River, lies an area where carnival music was once heard, merry-go-round carousel horses galloped in place, a rollercoaster roared, and Charleston dancers strutted their stuff. My auntie, actually my mother's first cousin, owned the place. In 1891, Drake (my mother's cousin) and his partner, Louis D. Wallace, established the Silver Beach Amusement and Realty Company with the intention of giving tourists something more to do in St. Joseph. Initially, ten cottages were built along the beach as rentals for vacationers. By the end of the amusement park's run, eighty cottages were available.

To make the cottages more popular to rent, Drake and Wallace invited local concessionaires to sell novelties such as swimming caps and lemonade in a barrel. Within months, games of chance and a photographic studio emerged to allow couples to have their portraits taken. By 1896, an ice cream parlor, souvenir shop, and a pavilion to host dancing and a big band music stand were erected. Wooden stands and white tents could be seen up and down the beachfront. A couple of water slides were anchored in shallow water for children around the turn of the century. This marked the beginning of the Silver Beach Amusement Park.

I spent every summer set loose among the carnies. Auntie was my idol. With dyed jet-black hair in a huge beehive and an ever-present cigarette hanging from her painted red lips, she was diametrically opposed to my straitlaced parents. She drank whiskey like a man, swore like a pirate, and ran that amusement park with the ease of a dictator. I adored her.

So what was a little game of bumper cars in a Podunk town in France? I had ridden with the best. Apparently the cars in France are not regulated as to speed or severity of impact, however, and our little blond boy was rammed by an adult, practically thrown from the car, and bit through his tongue. We got back to the Maison des Mouches, and the neighbor called the doctor. House calls, too! The doctor spoke no English, yet we understood his words: *un chirurgien*, a surgeon must be found.

As we trundled the countryside in search of the hospital, the car exuded an eerie quiet. The hospital, after midnight, echoed our isolation as we called out to the empty hallways for help. A lone doctor with passable English found us lost in the corridors and ushered us into the examination room. He mimicked stitching in a fast game of charades, and off Reg, boy, and doctor went, ostensibly to the sewing room. I followed along, only to be stopped at the door. "*Pas mère*" was audible. I didn't understand the language, but I knew a body block when I saw one. I was incensed! What type of establishment didn't allow the mother of the child to enter the sewing room? As I reflect on that question, the answer was probably most first-world countries that have even a brief smattering of the understanding of mother-child relationships. Thirty minutes later the trio emerged, stitched and smiling. I had not been stitched and I certainly wasn't smiling, but we were free to go with the entire bill of $20 to be sent to our home in California. They didn't even ask if we had insurance before the procedure. Scooter recovered quickly. I'm not sure why it takes parents longer.

11:28 Home
Had a great time
Thanks.
Love
—Scooter

This was the child who, should you need anything, say on a trip to Kenya or Antarctica—a toothpick, dental floss, or a needle and thread—could produce it from a fanny pack in a quick second, or say, "I'll be right back," and arrive in minutes with your request granted. Napkins for runny ice cream—got it! An extra toothbrush and toothpaste—got it! I didn't ask him if he could procure a tampon for me, but I was tempted. It was like magic, and he soon became a family legend.

Once he accidentally locked us out of a home we were trading in Scotland. Being foreigners, we didn't know where to turn. Mr. Pick-a-Lock fashioned, out of a stick, a way to open the inside storm door after locking us out of the front door. There was probably a gap of at least three feet between the doors, and it was getting to be a cold winter night. But he did it!

Of course, when I asked him to produce better grades, he smiled that smile that melted hearts and said nothing. Years later, when he turned his life around, he had to take a series of tests to qualify for the intense military training program he was enlisting in and missed one answer. I asked him why he hadn't used his high intellect at a younger age, and his answer was, "Then I would have had to work. This way I got by until I decided what I wanted to do with my life."

I should have known between the Lego pieces that were missing in the complex design, to the computer parts that had been strewn all over the room in the quest to figure out how the damn thing worked, that his brain worked differently from others', and it was to be celebrated rather than attempting to smash his round peg into a square hole that he would never fit.

This is why I have grey hair.

～✐～

Hey party was fun
—Love Scooter

In elementary and middle school, he was shunned by other children. Their parents were cruel, looking aside and gathering their perfect children to the breast when the wild child entered the playground or public area. He could be so very sweet; it was heartbreaking for me to see the righteous indignation from across the jungle gym. Rarely was he invited to his classmates' parties. He knew he was not included yet didn't understand why.

Schools changed, sometimes yearly and sometimes during the middle of the year, in an earnest search for a place to fit. During a two-year time frame, he went from the most expensive private preschool, kindergarten, and first grade in the county to the local parochial school for second and third grade, to a three-day-a-week charter school for a few months, and finally a Montessori school that worked best for his personality—for a month. His choice would have been the charter school, as it involved only three days in the classroom, and he enjoyed knitting, weaving, and art. I didn't mind the knitting, weaving, or art, but the three-day school week did me in. I was working seven days a week and couldn't leave him at home to fend for himself. Bringing him to work was out of the question, as the mothers of my students didn't want him around. I was in the classroom, doors closed, to concentrate on my dance students and couldn't watch him and properly teach. He attended the charter school for a few months and Montessori for a month before being asked to leave. The last-ditch attempt was public school, having run the gambit of all other options.

Then and now, I feel the same way. Public school is great for middle-of-the-road and higher-achieving students. Teachers are accustomed to dealing with those levels. It is when you throw a child with learning differences and emotional issues into that student base that problems arise. Scooter wasn't categorized with the kind term "learning differences." Instead he was labeled a troublemaker, destined to live on the radar of the administration as a problem to be dealt with—and not in a manner best suited for him. Choices were few to none.

Today there are no more children with learning differences than there were when my children grew up; they existed in a classroom then as they do today. The acceptance of these children has become normal. The physically, emotionally, and otherwise challenged child has become the parent of challenging children, and perhaps part of the change is due to the hurtful memories these parents harbor.

His first year of public school, fifth grade, was a wonderful and surprising year. The teacher was just like Scooter, ADD all over, and my boy thrived. Anyone walking into the classroom could see there was a different vibe. Airplane models hung from the ceiling at various levels, with no rhyme or reason to their placement. The desks were an organized mess with no patrol designed to create order. Chaos reigned in discussions, and for the first time in eight years of school, Scooter really wanted to engage in the classroom. He wanted to please that teacher. He was a stellar student and would maintain forever that Mr. Patrick was the best teacher in the world. Unfortunately, that year was over quickly.

There was an independent program in grades six through eight that I tried in vain to enroll him in. It would have allowed for discretion regarding testing and homework, but the district-appointed psychologist wouldn't accept my plea and believed Scooter was fine just where he was. His troublemaking behavior trumped a potential learning difference, and he slid slowly through the cracks of the educational system. I knew he wasn't fine. When sixth grade started, his depression worsened by the day. He was bored and depressed and bereft of friends. He muddled through sixth grade at the huge and scary middle school. That was not his assessment, it was mine. I empathized. I went to the campus myself and was immediately overwhelmed. There were people everywhere. A band was playing in a corner, taco booths and pizza tables were hawking their goods, people were reading poetry, and there was a general din of 586 captive teenagers waiting to pounce—on the pizza, a taco, each other, or me.

In seventh grade, he decided the best way to make friends was to share his Dexedrine with six of his close and personal school chums. Fortunately, none of the other children were harmed, but Scooter was implicated immediately, and I was summoned. Suspension from school followed shortly, and he was ordered to enter a local psychological testing program.

The night before he was supposed to attend his first day of a six-week program, he sliced the inside of his wrists and then wrapped them up in bandages and hid his arms in the sleeves of his hoodie as we left for the first intake meeting. As soon as we got there, he was ushered away from me, and I was none the wiser about what had been a legitimate suicide attempt by an eleven-year-old boy. I'd been alerted that there would be a forty-five-minute intake period, but after two hours, I was worried and haranguing the secretary about what was taking so long.

There were no acceptable answers to my questions until I was summoned into a cramped office away from the formal reception area. A physician, a psychologist, and I took a deep breath and simply stared at each other for a moment. Then, with a sharp tone, the physician asked me if I knew my son had attempted suicide the night before.

Stunned and without missing a beat, my reaction was akin to a mother bear facing a potential cub abduction; my voice rose by an octave and I felt physically ill. *Do you think I would have brought him in if I had known? Or at least I would have acknowledged it. More likely we'd be at the hospital!* Questioning and accusatory eyes seemed to glaze over with my protestations. I was on trial. It wasn't the first time.

I was informed that potential suicides take longer than regular intakes, and that was the reason for the long wait. My chagrin, fear, embarrassment, concern, and inadequacy bubbled over into a state of shock when Scooter showed me his knife work. "How could you have not known?" they asked. My own mind was light years ahead of their accusations and borderline taunts. After years of blaming myself anyway, why should this be different?

There was so much under the surface of this young teen, so much pain and abandonment. I had no idea. This single culminating event of a botched suicide, brought on by a series of events over the years, was the pivotal moment, tipping the scale of the future. No longer could I make excuses about the anger, depression, and avoidance. No longer could I pretend it was a phase. No longer was my world known to me. An unknown door had been opened, and the demons that held it open were also pushing me through the entrance whether I wanted to go or not. I was aware that a portal to hell had been opened, and now solutions had to be found.

This program that discovered the suicide attempt offered a six-week interim option during regular school hours to facilitate a buffer from the public school and time to find a decision for Scooter's future.

Educational consultant expertise was sought, and two programs seemed to fit Scooter's needs: a summer program that would segue into a year-round school in Montana. The cost would be mine to bear. With monthly fees close to $6,000, the only way forward was to refinance the house. Scooter's father blamed me and would contribute nothing to a solution, monetarily or emotionally. I panicked at the thought of finding that kind of resource, but Reg simply stated a fact: "Do you want to find the money it's going to take to save him, or do you want to pay for a funeral?" I never answered that question out loud. We refinanced.

I'm back and alive.
—Scooter

After the suicide attempt, we got very serious, very quickly. Educational specialists in Palo Alto were recommended and consulted. While we awaited appointments, he couldn't go back to school, so there was a school program at the actors' recovery center that kept him busy in the mornings. For a couple of years, Reg had been threatening military boarding school, but those ideas were feeble attempts to right destructive behavior. Nothing worked. His room had become his cave and his solace. Golf lessons, bay sailing outings, and finally scuba lessons were introduced to keep him busy, yet there wasn't too much that captured his imagination or desire.

It was an interesting fact that he possessed great hand-to-eye coordination, so sports came quite easily but didn't engage him. To our credit, we tried many outlets but couldn't hit any homeruns. The tried-and-true video games, played in the dark into the wee hours of the morning, were all that mattered to Scooter. While we looked for answers for schooling, we gave in to his world. We'd reached the end of our patience. He was interviewed, tested, retested, and reinterviewed. We were interviewed, psychoanalyzed, therapized, and terrorized. Why was this happening? We had no answers.

The final assessment suggested a six-week outdoor camp in Idaho that would allow for consultants to delve deeper into the type of year-round schooling that would be most beneficial. To their credit and in hindsight, this mother/son Bay Area team were professional, skilled in their field, kind, and supportive.

Early one cold morning, Reg awakened Scooter from his sleep and requested he get dressed and pack his backpack with only the essentials for an overnight. They were going on a trip. They went to the airport and caught a plane to Idaho where, waiting at the gate, were the representatives from the outdoor program. The program administration knew from experience that the mother was not the best candidate for "transportation companion," so my going along on the drop-off wasn't an option.

About fifteen minutes before the plane landed, Reg gently informed my son that he would be staying, and that Reg would be returning to Monterey on the next flight. Apparently in somewhat of a daze of misunderstanding, Scooter's only question was, "Will I be home tonight?"

Reg delivered the boy to the reps and turned to find a pay phone. He fell apart, crying while trying to talk to me. He would contend for many years to come that this was the most difficult thing he ever had to do.

Days later, there was a phone call from the outdoor program officials. We had been warned about the typical rhetoric. He would beg to come home and say he would do anything we asked if he could return. This information was relayed from a counselor, and we were not allowed to talk to him for the entire six weeks. Peace and silence in the home was the outward blessing of his absence, yet tranquility masked tragic feelings of guilt. How could I be happier when he was not at home? It was a stark reality; we were all better off, including Scooter.

At the end of the six-week program, we had made a plan: he would be segued to a program in Montana for the year. We had gone from military to therapeutic in six weeks. He didn't need an extremely regimented school, and the statistics supported the conclusion that a therapeutic environment would help him heal.

A stunning fact: researchers at Duke University found that 68 percent of children under age sixteen had exposure to at least one traumatic event, but it's also true that kids under age seven were unreported. In fact this number is likely higher. Consequently, the majority of us are vulnerable to latent mental issues, including not just suppressed traumatic stress, but pent-up rage that can lead to crippling anxieties, dysfunctional depression, and self-defeating behaviors. This rage, of course, is also at the heart of our hatred toward others. We externalize the unremitting pressure from within. Scooter didn't need a uniform; he needed guidance and support.

After three months, the Montana school had a hundred-mile father-son kayaking trip, which Reg, being an outdoor man, was attracted to on many levels. The ex-marine in him could handle any battle with expectations of success, and he really thought he could "fix" Scooter's problems. There continued to be no maternal options for visitation. With the prospect of a kayak trip without a shower or bathroom for ten days, I was grateful not to have been included. Reg happily signed up. At that time, Scooter's father was nearly seventy-five and in poor health, which disqualified him from the experience. Since the paternal side of the family thought I was the reason for the boy's inability to cope, it was essentially all my fault and therefore mine to deal with.

I was left waiting almost nine months before I had an opportunity to see my son. The last sighting I remembered was in the dark of a winter morning, closing the door on Reg and Scooter as they left for the airport. Nine months later, when I was finally invited to visit, the plane trip I took alone was one of excitement dampened by trepidation and tinged with unknowns. Would Scooter welcome or vilify me; would he be changed; was there hope? He was on "solo," meaning in a tent out in the wilderness, left alone for three to four days at a time with a ration of food to last that time. If he ate it all in one day, too bad.

The counselor led me out to his tent. I don't think he knew I was coming. I was elated to finally see him. Physically he was taller and leaner, and clearly, he was emotionally stronger with his open welcome, eagerness to talk about his life, and genuine concern for the well-being of his siblings. I couldn't allow my enthusiasm for evidence of permanent change to cloud the obvious; he had a ways to go. Had we known it would be another twelve to fourteen years before we could see the light in his eyes, maybe I would have cried uncle, but we didn't have a crystal ball. We kept on because that's what you do when you don't know anything else to do. His note about being back and alive is most poignant.

Happy Day after Easter!
First note of weekend home for a visit!
Had lots of fun
Home safe
Love,
—Scooter

Within the program Scooter attended in the Montana backwoods, students were required to "earn" back what most of us take for granted. By attending required therapy sessions, study halls, and successfully finishing chores, the students earned rights. The first right to be earned was a move from a tent in the yard to a bed in the house. The house was a rambling, three-story, five-thousand-square-foot, custom-built log cabin. It took Scooter eight months to earn the right to have a real roof over his head. I'm not sure exactly when he realized he had no choice but to follow the program in order to return to his California home, yet as the months went by, he acclimated to the repetitive daily life and began to flourish with structure and rules. It was the spring before his senior year in high school. His grades were better than ever, and he had earned to right to come home for a weekend. It was the first weekend that he'd been allowed to fly on his own, and I had not been privy to the plan. Reg had gone out under the guise of needing to pick something up at the market. I wasn't sure what had been forgotten, but I was busy with Easter dinner and didn't pay too much attention to the comings and goings of the rest of the family.

I was deep in the process of creating a traditional Easter meal—leg of lamb, mashed potatoes, carrots, and asparagus—when the doorbell rang and I went to the gate. There he stood, wearing ridiculous pink bunny ears strapped to a headband and a huge, somewhat goofy smile. Reg stood proudly beside him, sporting his own pair of pink ears. My sweet husband had arranged this reunion, and I was beyond surprised and delighted. Holidays were a very special time, filled with decorations and much planning. To have my children with me, all of them, was the ultimate gift. This was what I learned when one was not there, year after year—that the most precious gift is family, especially when it also contains peace.

Now he wanted our permission to come home for his senior year. I told him it would be social suicide, but his insistence that he had accomplished all of the goals he had been assigned was hard to argue with. My anxiety over a relapse, depression, failing grades, or worse—another suicide attempt—was through the roof. But he had done everything that had been asked of him. He pointed that out in a quiet, adult fashion. It was our turn to trust.

Happy New Year!
First note of 2002!
Had lots of fun
Home safe
Love,
—Scooter

Arrive home he did. He completed his year with somewhat less stellar grades than his junior year, but since we hadn't set our sights on MIT, and he wasn't graduating in the bottom fifth of his class, we were thrilled.

It was odd having him settle into home again, but without the daily anger and outbursts. He focused his newfound therapeutic skills on this sister, four years his junior. Since her eyeball-rolling ability was arguably the best in the family, he set about trying to reason with her. Have you ever tried to reason with a thirteen-year-old? Yet, he was persistent. They would disappear into the bedroom for hours at a time, attempting to come to resolution of a problem, only to appear finally, after being called numerous times for dinner, frustrated and unresolved. He didn't give up, though. They ended up having a good relationship once she got out of high school, though she was always a bit wary, knowing he had the experience to see through her idiosyncratic excuses.

11:00 p.m.
Home
Went to Borders and bought a magazine
Goodnight
—Scooter

The best part about the children driving was that I no longer had to. They were happy to run small errands: the dry cleaner, the grocery, the pet store, and other mind-numbing stops as long as it entailed getting behind the wheel.

The afternoon of the bookstore, I had sent him to the post office right before it closed. I am a letter writer from way back. I do hand write thank-you notes on Crane paper with a beautiful pen—a lost art. It is something my mother did, and I learned from her that a person didn't use a gift until the thank-you had been written and mailed. I wrote thousands of notes over my business career, especially to young people. Many of them had never gotten a real letter in the mail. Imagine!

On this particular mission to the post office, I had over a dozen letters to mail and I gave him a $10 bill. When he got home, he handed me $9.88. I asked him why he gave me back so much money.

He said, "Why would I pay thirty-seven cents for a stamp when they sell them for a penny?"

Well, the logic was sound, I had to admit, but the reality didn't align with the logic. All the notes were returned for postage due the following week. He obviously had been living in the Montana outback for too long. I resolved to give better instructions next time.

Prom 2003
Hey I'm home
Had lots of fun!
Thank you very much
Goodnight
—Scooter

I couldn't believe I was witnessing something as normal as a prom. The lack of what is considered normal or typical as opposed to abnormal or downright scary behavior had been recalibrated in our family. Sleepovers and experiments with makeup and first kisses had been replaced with ER visits and close acquaintance with the various well-known shrinks in town.

Where did the innocence go? Back in my day, the most scandalous outings were called "Come as you are" parties. This form of entertainment was the rage when I was a preteen, back in the days of the dinosaurs. When you got the call, always close to bedtime, to come to the party that weekend, whatever you were wearing at the time you answered the call was your party attire. My mother would always make me change my pajamas before answering the phone. At the time, I didn't think it was odd, not any odder than some of her other stunts, yet after a couple of these "scandalous parties," I understood her motive. It didn't have much to do with what you wore to the party; it was more about her need to control a situation. Other girls would come as they were when they answered the phone, hair rolled in orange juice cans and old pajamas. Not me. Rosemary had zipped up that problem and managed the outcome. I just figured their mothers didn't care about them as much as mine did.

I never knew if my other friends had such thoughtful and obsessive mothers. I am damn proud of my inherited desire for perfection, and I don't know why my children think there is something wrong with this trait. Nowadays, kids go to school in their Hello Kitty pajama bottoms and fluffy slippers, so the intrigue has gone right out of that party theme.

The prom is normal, right? I was even requested to attend the fitting at Men's Wearhouse for the tuxedo. Not my choice, but I was learning to keep my mouth shut as I had been invited. There was too much powder blue, a hat of questionable taste, and a slight western edge that made my head turn slightly while I tried not to look like a disgruntled poodle. I was able to order the girl's corsage without comment. Photos were taken. The date was sweet looking, and a good time was had by all. A normal evening, for a prom. It is a happy memory.

◠◡◠

I'm safe, sober and it was fun.
Now I'm going to sleep.
—*Scooter*

He didn't stop taking the Adderall until he was eighteen, when he finally refused to continue against the doctor's suggestion.

At that time, higher education wasn't something he was interested in, so we tried to find something he wanted to do. Reg was on the board of trustees at a Chinese university five hundred miles north of Beijing. Quite a way from Beijing; China is a huge country. Reg and I had visited, and it came as a revelation to me. Why not spend a year at the university and learn Mandarin? Perhaps Scooter would find an entrepreneurial thread in his personality and become a successful businessman. Scooter jumped at the chance to do something very different from his older brother. China was perfect. I figured he couldn't compete with his textbook-brilliant brother, so he needed a different continent. Just how much trouble can one student get into in a foreign county, not just foreign, but Communist foreign? He didn't end up in jail, and in his freshman year of studies, he majored in girls, barroom Chinese, and giving cooking lessons.

Turns out he not only didn't get into trouble. He fit in. Bloom where you are planted! In no time, he figured out the classes were being taught by underpaid US and foreign-born Christian missionaries, and they would pay a small Chinese fortune for jade crosses to adorn their sainted necks while doing the work of the Lord among thousands of heathens. So our boy, Mr. Entrepreneur, got a shady contact and up-charged to make sure he had enough money for beer and vodka at the local bar. His cheese fry classes at the bar were a real hit, and he then moved on to basic hamburgers and variations on American sandwiches, like the BLT. Of course, the B preceding the L and the T could have been a bit questionable in China, but once fried, what the heck?

Between jewelry sales and cooking classes, the only thing he could have added to the equation was tobacco sales. His one-man hedonistic business sense kept him from asking for spending money, allowing the parental bank a respite, albeit brief, from oiling the printing press.

So what was missing in his life? You've got the food, the booze, the ciggies, and hmm . . . let me think. A woman. Well, he got one of those, too: a lovely Honduran woman, six years his senior and a teacher at the university—a Christian missionary teacher hooking up with the ultimate pagan worshipper: drugs, sex, and Techno music. She wanted the marriage made in heaven, so he brought her back to us for our blessing. She was warm and caring, knew how to win our affection, had obviously won his affection, and couldn't have been more wrong for him. He was a nineteen-year-old boy, and she was a woman with a mission: to get a green card. Not that I didn't believe she loved my crazy middle boy. Really, who wouldn't? He was the life of the party, honest to a fault, and a cross between a golden retriever and a bulldog—of course resembling the golden and the spirit of the breed's name. They went on and off, for almost eleven years—mostly off, yet never really cutting the cord. She was his first love. It hurt for him to say goodbye, yet her religious fervor and born-again beliefs were incompatible with his agnostic attitude. Sometimes things don't work out. I have found that timing in life has everything to do with stars not aligning—the wrong place at the right time, or the other way around.

Hey, I'm home
Doors are locked
Alarm is on
Thanx for letting
me use the car
—Scooter

"No matter how much you try to hold onto something,
it will all be gone."
—Taoist proverb

Doors are locked and the alarm is on, yet they still get away. One of the most profound experiences in being a parent is realizing the entire reason you raise children is to let them go. This is a fact that parents of newborns should have broadcast daily into their brains. I envision a chip implant that plays stereo in their heads reinforcing the fact that these are the good days. One day you will miss these times, and one day you will welcome the chance to spoil your grandchildren while attempting to juggle explosive diarrhea diapers, teething, colic-ridden two in the morning fits, and vomiting, fever-induced trips to the ER. We are raising them to leave us. Oh, yes, they will be productive, hopefully, and not incarcerated for murder, but the entire purpose of having children is to get rid of them. I have been witness to and actually been a parent who had difficulties conceiving a child. Upon their arrival, you couldn't have knocked the stars out of my eyes with a two-by-four because I hadn't realized the inevitable.

By the time eighteen or thirty years have passed, that reality is yours to reflect upon. But some kids go the opposite direction. It's an international phenomenon—kids who won't go away. The Italians call them *mammon*, or "mama's boys." The Japanese call them *parasaito shinguru*, or "parasite singles." In the United States, they are known as boomerangs, and in the United Kingdom, they're called KIPPERS—"Kids In Parents' Pockets Eroding Retirement Savings."

According to 2016 data, close to 32 percent of Americans aged eighteen through thirty-four were living with their parents. If we expand this category to include those living with relatives outside of their immediate family, the statistic rises to almost 40 percent. Generally speaking, this is a more common practice for sons than daughters. Surveys in the United Kingdom and Japan suggest a similar situation in those countries. Hey, growing up is hard to do. If you stay at home, someone else is paying the mortgage, shopping for food, and cooking it. Services may include the laundry as well. It's as if there is a butler, maid, cook, and housekeeper—all for the low cost of a couple hundred dollars a month rent, if the parents are even that insistent. Tough love means kicking kids out of the nest and letting them learn for themselves. Not only are they born to leave, they are born for us to heave them, ready or not, into the wild abyss of the unnatural world. Why on earth did we sign up for this duty?

2:00 a.m.
The concert
was awesome!
Thanks
Love
—Scooter

The beat emanating through the floor from the upstairs bedroom included a mélange of club remix, new beat, and Detroit Techno . . . usually a repetitive, repetitive, repetitive instrumental sound, heavy on the bass. Now, I try not to be a fuddy-duddy, but I've never been able to tell one part of this beat from another where my kids' music is concerned. I just stand and bob my head to the incessant sameness and look like I'm cool.

There is no spiritual awakening like there was to the music of the '60s and '70s. There have been studies on how young people today relate to the music of my era. There is a remarkable affinity for the music of the '60s, yet the folks studying this phenomenon believe it's due to grandparents playing the moldy oldies for the rug rats, which produced a nostalgic feeling toward the grand folks and therefore toward their music.

For me, music isn't what it used to be when there were records. My first recording was a coral pink 45 of Debbie Reynolds singing "Tammy." I graduated from the soft soap love songs to the hard realities of the '60s, Woodstock to Vietnam. I proudly embraced ZZ Top, having cut my eye teeth in South Texas, and always thought that early Rolling Stones by far beat the soft sounds of the Beatles. I do remember seeing *A Hard Day's Night* at the movie theatre. I was ten years old and screamed at the screen like the rest of the predominately pre-teen audience. I am quite sure I didn't know what I was screaming about. My generation of young girls liked Beatles music, but it was more about their looks. They were racy in a clean-cut way. Of course, the hair! That put our parents over the edge. We loved that the most. Who today isn't well-versed in Beatles compositions? Who is going to remember the 2006 Best of Techno Martin Buttrich? Or his choice to be silent studio partner on Loco Dice's "Seeing Through Shadows," with its acidic bass line that you could dance to forever? Spare me. I didn't share much about my own music with my children until I heard strains of "Dream On," by that hardcore boy toy Steven Tyler, or "White Rabbit," a Grace Slick epic; only, then, a short story about my not-so-pure past was in order.

~

Hey, Hey, Hey
It's a new world out here
Love you
—Scooter

He realized four years away had changed everything he had once known. Four years in the safety of a bubble was over. He didn't let on that he was scared, and neither did I.

Cinnamon

Cinnamon: December 5, 1987

Eyes: Blue

Hair: Blond

The baby, hell bent on not being left behind; dreamer; immature; adept at getting others to do things for her.

"Dreamers can't be tamed."
—Paul Coelho

Hi, it's 11:00
Home safe
Love you
Sleep well
—Cinnamon

Her brothers called her "baby ala boo," which made her laugh. Her blue eyes were the only vestige of her father—the boys have my browns. At five years old, she told me she was going to live on a faraway continent on seven thousand acres of inherited land and save endangered animals. I told her I supported her completely, though I was a bit concerned about the inherited part. Ancestry.com claims we are of German descendants, so the chances of finding a relative to inherit land from on the African continent might be considered a bit farfetched. Parents are cautioned not to cast any disparaging comments on the dreams of youth. So while she dreamed of saving the planet, I prayed for no skinned knees, hospital trips, or issues requiring stitches or casts.

From a note left on top of the laundry basket:
I didn't know
if you wanted these
cleaned so, I didn't
put them in. I thought
they could just need to
be folded.
I love you!
—Cinnamon

For a single mom living in an eight-hundred-square-foot, one-bedroom apartment with three children and no washer/dryer, the public Laundromat was a biweekly outing. I knew the last load had to be into the machine by nine o'clock. I would get off work at eight thirty and dash to make the deadline. The establishment was only a few blocks away, so I would lock the children in and rush off to make clean clothes. Picture a black convertible Corvette with laundry from three children piling out of the open top. After too many weeks of seeing the same clothes, still folded, in the dirty clothes hamper, I finally got savvy. They were simply not putting the clean, folded clothes in the drawer to be worn and then washed. Instead of finding their home in the clean clothes drawer, someone was simply putting the clean clothes back in the hamper to be endlessly washed without wearing. This behavior was traced to Cinnamon, who, instead of telling me not to buy something because she didn't like it and ultimately wouldn't wear it, simply said, "Great," to my clothing taste—and then did what she wanted. This manner of recycling, though ingenious on one hand, only served to irritate. When I become upset, it's probably best for everyone to clear the room.

One of my many flaws is a delayed reaction to the buildup of irritations. I have been likened to a Vulcanian eruption with explosions like cannon fire: ash and fallout spreading over acres of surrounding lands and extinction of everything in a multiple-mile radius. Cue my temper tantrum.

Recycling issue fixed.

A simple project like laundry is taken for granted by most people living in a first-world country. With three children, even without the Cinnamon-style wash, there are simply tons to be done. It wasn't long before I asked my mother to buy me a washer and dryer. Fortunately, she came through.

To the world, you may be
one person; but to one person
you may be the world. . . .
—*Cinnamon*

Enjoy the sentiment of a note like this while you can. Soon you will be the most despised individual in the world. All you must do is remember how you felt about your mother and then, if she is still around, apologize.

Daughters are a gift from ages zero to ten, and then after twenty-two.

The in-between is a hormonal journey through Dante's nine circles of hell. Be very afraid! One day your adorable daughter will flip from a little girl in pigtails into a full-blown adult discussion with your spouse regarding the wisdom of conception at any cost. If you deny that you've had this discussion/argument, you are lying to yourself. The scary fact of surfacing bad and entitled attitudes is the reality of witnessing this behavior in young children. I have heard five-years-olds who are proficient. My daughter's first eyeball roll was recorded at age six, while trash duty was being meted out. It was a classic roll, no embellishment, yet it seemed highly precocious at the time.

Perfecting the art of eyeball rolling was born at the feet of a prepubescent teenage girl somewhere back in the Dark Ages. Today, eyeball rolling doesn't mean what it did a hundred years ago. Percentage-wise, girls eyeball roll more than boys. Boys get aggressive in the preteen years and shove, push, and posture. Girls show their contempt by facial expressions.

There are references to eye-rolling in Shakespeare and throughout literature as far back as the fifteenth century. Eye-rolling was thought to be a look of passion and lust. In the eighteenth and nineteenth centuries, rolling one's eyes could signal danger, flirtation, or loving affection. Until the 1950s, when eyeball rolling began to take on today's connotation of extreme boredom and unbelievable scorn, one's eyeball exercise might have meant you were sad and lugubrious, sexually wanton, or totally indifferent. Who could forget reading the classic *Where the Wild Things Are* by the late Maurice Sendak: "And the wild things roared their terrible roars and gnashed their terrible teeth and rolled their terrible eyes and showed their terrible claws."

Apologies for potentially ruining a perfectly good children's book with the reality of your bored pre-tween.

Hello! It is 11:55. I am home.
Thank you for letting me go out. I'm truly sorry for
not thinking
last night. I love you
Sleep well
—Cinnamon

Always forgive and give another chance . . . to hang themselves. You know it's only a matter of time.

My children were never accused of being impolite. I was raised by a Southern mother, so they learned their manners at a young age. All three were able to hide behind that screen of devious and graceful formality until the inevitable great reveal of guilt and shame. It has been a lifelong study in charming manipulation. They always knew they would be guilty before proven innocent. I truly believe the little darlings conspire to drive us over the edge from their first breath to our last. When's the last time a mother, when repeatedly told to rest when her newborn rests, actually rests? She gets up, does the laundry, cleans the house, and makes a casserole.

Many parents believe their child wouldn't bully, curse, or be destructive to the property of others. Their children would never make another child cry. Are these the mothers with the perfect wardrobe, shoes, and handbags? And fathers tolerate aggressive male patterns. Are they kidding? If aliens visited, they might observe the destructive consequences of bullying behavior at the highest levels of our current society. When young people attempt to fit into the cool crowd, be accepted by their peers, or otherwise not stand out in school or social situations, they can be driven by the base impulse to belittle or physically hurt. Cinnamon was targeted for her weight gain at age six, which made her totally uncool. She withdrew, Scooter fought back. She was called Fatty McFatty, and Scooter was taunted until a fistfight erupted.

Today, with the advent of the cyber world, bullying has taken on life-threatening consequences. Bullying is not itself a new phenomenon—the verb first came into use in the 1700s, and the act it describes originated even earlier than that. But in recent years, it has taken on a new sense of urgency and significance. This is due in some part to the aforementioned rash of "bully-cides" (suicides caused by bullying), but also to what some have called the general "epidemic" of bullying. Our children are being raised in a very different world from their parents.

I am home
Safe and sound!
I love you
Sleep well!
—Cinnamon

Of course she loves me. I'm asleep.

Don't you remember creeping into your children's rooms once they were asleep? You gently pulled the covers up to their chin and ran your hand through their hair. You thanked God for this blessing.

Please don't let that memory be tarnished; yet, do remember, *they were asleep!* Children become angels when at rest.

My daughter always said she would be the one to take care of me in my dotage, but that would not come to pass since she moved to South Africa at age eighteen, with no intention to return. Nine of those years, she pursued her dream of saving wild cats. In 2008, we visited her in the lodge where she worked and were treated to five-hour jaunts to the bush, finding and discussing all manner of wild beasts from lions to elephants, rhinos to hippos. Her knowledge and growth amazed me.

During much of that time, she worked with a mentor whose knowledge of cheetahs allowed her lifelong dream of saving these magnificent creatures to come true. Her stories of life, death, and salvation for these cats were at once heartwarming, frightening, loving, and enlightening. She then moved on to a nonprofit organization whose goal was to teach the traditional South African farmer—typically older white, Dutch-bred, gun-toting, conservative men—how to deal with a leopard eating their sheep, without killing said cat.

Cinnamon found sexism alive and well in the patriarchal society of South Africa. After all, she was a little blond California chick telling *men* in South Africa what to do. My mother lives on in my daughter.

Her dream of becoming a farmer in South Africa would be fraught with stories we blessed folk in the good ol' USA don't hear too much about, like farm murders.

In total, between 1998 and the end of 2016, 1,848 people will be murdered in farm attacks—1,187 farmers, 490 family members, 147 farm employees, and 24 people who happened to be visiting the farm at the time.

While South Africa has one of the highest rates of violent crime anywhere in the world, the attacks on white farmers are no ordinary crimes. Any form of justice is incredibly rare, and white farmers are increasingly questioning their future. The number of commercial farmers in South Africa between between 1980 and 1997 dropped by 70,000, and by 2011 there were only 40,000 left. Thousands more farms are up for sale.

All that taken into account, Cinnamon's journey will continue. My knees are those of a pious, rosary-praying Catholic, skinned by the hard wooden pews. I think, *He is not listening.*

Hey
Got home after
Sarah's at 10:00 pm
Then went out with Laura
Be back before 12:30
I have my cell
—Cinnamon

I really want to impress this on mothers contemplating the inevitable: when to allow their daughters to date. I *highly* suggest no later than fourteen or fifteen. This only comes after a trip to the doctor for birth control, but there is more behind this idea than just the fear of pregnancy and STDs. They need to kiss their frogs and come to the family to boast, cry, vent, and grow. Once they are in college or on their life path after eighteen, when you *must* let go, it's too late. In high school, you still have a grip, albeit a white-knuckle one for the parental unit, but you have something to say, and they have to listen.

I remember my mother putting her finger against my ear. I didn't have a clue about what she was doing. Then she said, "Maybe if I close up one side of your hearing, something will stick inside." Funny how many times she was right; just sorry I didn't know it then. It would have saved a lot of heartache.

Cinnamon was a high school medal-winning jock and a dancer. She was so busy there wasn't time to date. That was my approach to child-rearing: submerse them in what they love, and they won't have time to get in trouble.

This is flawed thinking! You want them to get into trouble—hanging out with boys and having their peers bash and police them for even thinking about kissing that bad boy. If they've not been subjected to the harangue of a Valley Girl-voiced high school friend and her opinion, they've missed a life lesson worth learning: think twice to whom you listen for advice.

The issue with attempting to suppress the hormonal reality—what I thought was for the best—deposits an eighteen-year-old ragingly hormonal female into the world with absolutely no skills with the opposite sex and, in Cinnamon's case, landed her 10,237 miles (as the crow flies) from home, difficult to monitor and impossible to read. While I cannot use the word *disaster* for Cinnamon when it came to the boys-to-men department, I firmly believe that, had she dated in high school, she would have ferreted out the type of man she didn't want to be with and been able to sculpt the beginnings of the person she would allow herself to care about and with whom she could imagine a future existence.

Far better to make her mistakes in high school, where parents are there to talk to and discuss. Not making mistakes in high school leads to mistakes later that are more difficult to see if you don't have someone you trust to talk to.

> *It's 11:35. I am home safe and sound.*
> *I love you. Met a nice guy. I'll tell you about*
> *him tomorrow.*
> *—Cinnamon*

When the bundle is put on our tummy for inspection, we don't think about the possibilities of the bogeyman and his henchmen creating havoc. He can and he does. Some families talk about it, some don't. But many children suffer at the hands of pedophiles while the loving family is close by, watching and doing their job—or, they believe they are watching and doing their job. My daughter was sexually abused by a maintenance man who'd befriended the family. People were around, but he was surreptitious and sneaky. We didn't ask the right questions or see what was hidden.

She was just five. I was working long hours, attempting to hold the family together financially. I had hired a wonderful nanny who picked the kids up from school, did homework with them, fed them dinner, and got them to bed—all while I worked. She was with us five afternoons a week, but not on the weekends. I worked Saturday and Sunday, too.

I remember the maintenance man well. There were no signs of outward oddities. He was a "normal" thirty-plus, nice looking jack-of-all-trades. He had come recommended by a family friend, so that was good enough for me. There was always something to repair so he was frequently on the premises. When his cat had babies, he asked, ever so politely, if he could take Cinnamon to his home a few blocks away to see the kittens. I asked her if she wanted to go, and my little animal lover was overjoyed to be off to the babies. There was no trepidation on her part, so, as I look back, this could have been one of the early episodes. This horror lasted, by my best calculations after the fact, for at least a year. We aren't sure how many incidents, but we do know about him masturbating on her in the shower, digital penetration, and touching and feeling her body on numerous occasions.

I had taken a few days off after the Thanksgiving holiday, and upon return, late on Sunday evening, I encountered a partially comatose, partially freaked out nanny, rocking in a chair that wasn't meant for rocking, and staring into space.

My first reaction was an inquiry into whose death we would be attending to, when out of her mouth spewed a story that could not be made up. There was no doubt in this troubled woman's mind that the sexual abuse was underway in the moment she walked into the room to get Cinnamon. She was on his lap facing him, and her little panties were on the floor, his hands under her dress.

The nanny had caught him in the act and has probably never gotten over that moment. I imagine she blamed herself, yet there could be no blame placed except on the perpetrator. On some level, and statistically, the child blames herself for the abuse. She begins to act out, grades can drop, and she becomes more isolated. For Cinnamon, her reaction was to not want to be pretty anymore. My adorable little girl began to hoard cookies and sweets and to eat until she was overweight, and we were buying her clothes in the maternity area of the local department store. She demanded her waist-length hair be chopped off to Peter Pan length, and she stopped ballet.

Even though she had therapy immediately after the revelation, it wasn't until a new approach, eye movement desensitization and reprocessing (EMDR), was introduced to her at sixteen, that she felt a cloud lift, resulting in a real change in her attitude.

It was no wonder we had the three-month discussion about wearing a dress for First Holy Communion. Nothing closely resembling the pretty girl before five years old existed until she was almost eighteen.

Combine no dating with early sexual abuse, and it was not surprising she couldn't tell a bad relationship from a good one until close to her third decade.

Parents never really know the depth and breadth of the pain their child goes through as they grow and change with the lessons of life, regardless of happy memories or traumatic dissociation with feelings of unworthiness caused by catastrophic life issues. Not only did our family endure the heartbreak of abandonment issues surrounding a nasty divorce, we dealt with the aftermath of the most heinous crime against a child.

When my ex and his family learned of the abuse, there were two clear answers:

1) It was my fault for not being a stay-at-home mother and watching my children as a good mother should, and

2) his daughter, the woman I'd raised as my own, told me she was going to sue me for custody of my own children and prove I was an unfit mother.

So much for the support I was desperately seeking. That incident would end the relationship with my stepdaughter and strain the already tenuous father-daughter bond between Cinnamon and her biological father. I had to deal with the fallout from the abuse alone. Had I known his side of the family would be so unsupportive, perhaps I wouldn't have been so open about the abuse. Yet, that rejection made my conviction stronger.

Howdy!
It's 12:00 and I am
Home and safe
¡I love you!
Sleep well
—Cinnamon

It's hard to sleep when reality marches across the middle of the bed, day and night. Healing from the horror of abuse is a family issue, not limited to the abused.

I confronted the perpetrator, and, behind a wry smirk, he simply denied everything. I even called his mother. We all attended the same church. That difficult phone call only produced a venomous attack on me and my parenting skills. It was an impossible notion, and *bang* went the receiver.

We went directly to the chief of police in our small town, who was gentle, kind, and trained in these sordid matters. The typical anatomically correct doll helped her tell her story.

Counseling at the time included sand and play therapy. Since she was only six years old and we were considering prosecuting, we visited the courtroom for role-playing the potential hearing. She was told where she would sit and then where the accused would sit. She looked at the proximity of the two seats, and then looked at me and simply stated, "I can't do this."

At six years old, she had been through so much there was no question this was the end of the line. We went home and thought this was the end of a chapter. I knew it wasn't the end.

I am home . . . 11:15
The concert was fun
We went to Denny's
for a dessert
I love you
—Cinnamon

You heal and attempt to deal with the daily aftermath. Though I was distraught by the weight gain and the haircut, the isolation was the most difficult. To whom can you talk outside of the sanctity of the professional office? We hid the truth and didn't talk outside the family. The fact that it happened confirms the parents' worst fears—what a terrible parent I was, how I'd failed. Families and victims don't just need to talk—they need to yell at the top of their lungs, "I was abused and I won't let it happen to anyone else!"

It is easy to say and nearly impossible to do.

I looked at "intact" families and knew I had failed; failed to suck it up and therefore had to live the lie. There was no guilt in the heart of Mrs. Matching Handbag and Shoes, there was no guilt in the church deacon or in the Mother's Club president. Oh wait, that was me. I had enough guilt for everyone.

Everyone suffers from the Parade of the Horribles or the march of the guilty across the bed at two in the morning. I don't care how much you pray, light candles, or burn incense. The baby boomers are the generation that proclaimed loud and clear that we weren't going to do to our children what our parents had done to us. We had shelves in libraries and pages on Amazon dedicated to self-help, self-realization, and self-flagellation. We have Oprah, Dr. Phil, Steve Harvey, and Geraldo Rivera to let us know what failures we are and how to appeal to them for the answers to our guilt. Buy their books, get their DVDs, go to their seminars, repeat after me, hang mantras and prayer flags, take this, and do that. We were determined to un-fuck what had been fucked up.

We cannot grow from guilt. It is a self-fulfilling prophecy of internal hatred and shame. It is the battle cry of the condemned. Guilt doesn't allow you to sleep or eat well. It consumes the interior of your being and eats away, bit by bit, until exhaustion and, hopefully, good sense begin to take over. Exhaustion will allow you to sleep, and good sense will have an opportunity to knock on your thick skull and remind you that you are doing the best you can with the tools you've been given.

We cannot be above making mistakes. Parenting, at its best, is full of the need for self-correction and introspection. Had we known all of this, I am sure the brighter of the species would have begged off procreation many millennia ago.

We have heard that child-rearing is the most difficult job one can have, but we do not believe so we continue familial lineage. Therefore, we have children; we attempt to beat the odds that cannot be beaten.

⁓

I'm home. It's 11:40.
Sleep well. I love you.
Game was awesome. We won!
—Cinnamon

It took three months to get her into a dress for First Holy Communion. All femininity had been rejected. My being a girlie woman made this difficult for me, yet I knew she was trying to find her way back from the horror and devastating memories. This was not my battle or about me. I could stand by and love and support, but the battle was hers alone.

I wasn't always as supportive as I should have been, especially about hoarding food and overeating. After my initial thought—don't buy the stuff or have it in the house—I admit to words that, no doubt, still haunt her: "Why do you have to eat all the time? You are getting bigger." I had to juggle between feeding preteen boys who ate like locusts and having a daughter needing supervision. It's embarrassing today, yet I readily admit I didn't know what to do. I too had lost in this invisible disease of abuse. I had lost the innocence of my daughter and the opportunity to be a mom to a girl pretty in pink.

I was unavailable much of the time, and I have great understanding and empathy for single mothers worldwide. We can only do so much, and yes, our families may suffer as a result. Admitting it and moving forward is the only answer.

She took her angst and anger out on the sports field, where she excelled. Her tongue sharpened, and her demeanor shouted, "Don't mess with me." She starred on the soccer field and won awards and accolades for her huntress-style passion on the field.

She didn't just play sports; she was the MVP goalie on the field hockey team in high school. Field hockey goalies are a breed unto themselves. They stand next to their teammates, wearing pads and gear that totally disguise whether there is a boy or a girl underneath, while their teammates wear the tiniest of shorts or cute plaid miniskirts and matching fitted tank tops. While she never fit into skinny jeans, she had the strongest thighs and the calf muscles of a beauty queen. You need a strong constitution to be a field hockey goalie, as well as an intact ego to let go of the sight of a goalie running in her pads. She owned that high school sport, including the spirit of a warrior. She had fought since an early age to be heard, and she found her voice on the field.

By graduation, the baby fat and the cookie poundage had dropped off her five-foot-six-inch frame, and her waist-length hair was once again a crown.

We volunteered in a mother-daughter national organization that promoted philanthropy during her high school years. A specified number of volunteer hours needed to be logged each year. More hours were required of the young women to volunteer on their own and for the mothers to do the same—separate but equal. I joined thinking that when she hit the stage where she wouldn't want to either be seen with me or speak to me, we would still have to put up with each other picking up dog shit after an SPCA fundraiser. How could you not sign up for that duty? And to bond with your insolent, bitchy, griping fourteen-year-old at the same time? Sounds like a passage from Dante's *Inferno*. I was *so* in!

Not only was I in, but I was president of the local chapter for two years, as well as a district level officer. I was asked to go on to the national level, but she had graduated from high school by then. The dog shit patrol didn't hold as much joy without my sidekick.

Graduation, that was fun.

I got the phone call from the college placement guru at the $30,000-a-year prep school she attended to let me know a proud moment. She was to graduate in the bottom third of her class, but there was hope on the horizon, he added graciously, and a college fit for everyone.

Well, fuck that, I thought. Had she been the first child, I would have had an aneurysm on the spot. By the third one, it was more like, who cares, she'll find her way. Her way would be on a plane to a continent I'd never set foot on and a lifestyle as foreign to me as a life on easy street.

I am home. It is 1:30 . . . thank you for giving some extra time out.
Sleep well . . . I love you
—Cinnamon

Sometimes the family we are given is not the family we embrace. Oftentimes we can't see that when we are in their presence, we are home. Cinnamon found other male figures to give her what she craved, and fortunately, she found loving and caring individuals. Two were in the home—her protective brothers—and one came into the home: her stepfather. Another was a friend from her young years.

It wasn't until almost twenty years later that she grew to

love her stepfather. She had to leave, learn, fail, reach out, fail again, ask for more support, fail again, fall in and out of love at least a few times, ask for money again, have a baby, and ask for money again before she came to realize her stepfather was in it for the long haul.

In between, there were loving times, like when she slammed the door after her first visit home from the bush, screaming like an African primate, "I'm never setting foot in this house again!" And other loving times when she lowered her voice and hooded her eyes to spit out, "You're not my father." He does thank God for that blessing.

Then there were the other wonderful memories of driving her to school in the morning with her in stony silence for no apparent reason. There was no conversation, no "thanks for the ride," but at least also no "go to hell" (though I am sure that was a running dialogue with the good daughter/bad daughter that inhabited the same body for over five years of the treasured teenage years). I am told we have a tendency to remember the good times far more than the bad. Well, there you go!

During the kids' teenage years, I smoked cigarettes and drank my share of wine on a regular basis. Raising children during the times of hardcore brainwashing in school against both my treasured vices wasn't easy. I was the one harangued, spied on, and cursed for my horrible habits, goaded into hiding in the carport after dinner for a cig and a swig. Looking back at my self-inflicted misery, as I accept the total responsibility for the choices that led to me to a seven-day-a-week work existence on poverty level wages, doesn't make it any easier to have lived through it.

The brainwashing I endured as a young girl consisted of terrific tall tales surrounding the knight in shining armor who would arrive to save me from everything. That mantra began when I was fourteen and just entering high school. My answer to finding that knight was to borrow a book from the library on how to iron men's dress shirts properly. I can still wield a mean iron to this day. No knight in shining armor ever beat a trail to my door for a properly pressed pair of pants or a shirt, either. Perhaps I would have been better off learning a trade that valued WD-40.

Cinnamon's two older brothers would become my right and left arm, my middle-of-the-night phone call always taken, and my wakeup calls when I would feel the need to confess, I'd made tons of mistakes. They would love me and forgive me, despite my many, many shortcomings. She is still angry.

He who takes the child by the hand takes the Mother by the heart.
—*German proverb*

I am home, safe and sound. It's 10:50. Sleep well I love you. Do I have to fold the laundry? Scooter never does it!
—*Cinnamon*

It was the someday-to-be-husband's place to bring law and order to the Wild West. My home sweet homestead looked as though the posse had ridden into town, dropped the reins, used the facilities, forgotten to pay, and ridden off in a brewing lethal scandal. It looked that way from the outside and felt that way from the inside. The kids weren't asked to do much outside of decent grades—and even that wasn't happening. I thought that was their job and should be their only job.

Reg became the most hated sheriff in town. The atmosphere ranged from feigned indifference to expert eyeball rolling. I will say the laundry got folded, yet a week's worth of dishes were found on a regular basis, and hiding under the beds or behind computer screens were more used dishes that had failed to be put in the sink. As a single mother, I simply was far too tired to enforce any rules I might want, much less need. Left to their own devices, my children would have lived in continual squalor, and Cinnamon would be opening a rodent wing of the SPCA. Apparently, she had put out the word that she would help any friend with pets that were no longer wanted. Realizing she had a small space in which to run her rehab, she only accepted small creatures in cages. She grew used to the odors, a dusky mixture of leftover cat box and unwashed hamster homes. While collecting dishes, I realized something had possibly died in her room. I discovered her secret, and, by the next day, the cages were gone, all back to their original homes, safe and sound.

Yet our rodent issues were not over. Our one-eyed cat went totally ape shit one night, running into tables, scrabbling along the tile floor, and generally acting quite bizarre. It seems there was a loose mouse in the house, and in an attempt to be calm and accepting, as if I had learned a lesson from the caged visitors in Cinnamon's room, I suggested a humane trap so we could let the poor little dear go in the meadow behind the house.

The next day a trap was set and, in the morning, had a tenant. Out to the meadow the children somberly marched with the eviction notice.

A sweet calm prevailed over the cat—for twenty-four hours.

The next morning, I opened the cupboard to find an entire family of field mice having breakfast. Of course, I surprised them as much as they surprised me. The cat had a coronary, and I started to scream.

The humane trap was thrown into the trash can, followed by a phone call to "the guy" as he was fondly known in our family, who dealt with a variety of household catastrophes. I told the guy with the oversized spider on the side of his truck, in no uncertain terms, that this was not to continue. Spare no expense!

After openings in the house had been hermetically sealed per my instruction, actually with chicken wire, our mouse infestation was a story relegated to the past.

It is easy to start a family, but difficult to maintain it.
—Tibetan proverb

How are we ever going to live with Ashton? The pasta
deal was really too much.
It's 11:05
Sleep well
—Cinnamon

The firstborn was home from his first year at university. Pasta was on the table, and we were attempting to have a normal family dinner. This goal in itself was herculean. He started talking about *paaasta,* the way a Brit would pronounce it.

Cinnamon, not one to keep quiet, reserved, or diplomatic, lambasted her older brother. "You mean to say you spent a year in Italy and four months in the UK? It is pasta, not paaasta."

He huffed and puffed and finally relinquished the hard A sound, yet not without a bit of snobbery. No wonder the Brits have a snooty reputation.

It really didn't matter if we had company or not. My children did not adhere to the little-known carried-over child-rearing belief that children should be seen and not heard. My mother asked me constantly when my children were little, "Can't they be quiet?" They irritated her from the beginning as they refused to call her *Grand-mère,* but called her Grandma instead. The little heathens didn't realize she was an "heiress" by her standards, and hers alone. If she had been, I would have beaten the little heathens into submission as well, but she wasn't, and I chose my battles.

The boys had always remarked her meanness had skipped a generation, meaning right from grandma to granddaughter. Both Granny and the kid had tongues akin to a dull knife; they cut like hell and hurt a lot worse than a clean slice.

We all laughed about Cinnamon's edge, yet it was filled with a raw pain that gnawed at my base desire to keep everyone happy. There were the looks, the one-liners, and the rants. She was competitive on the field, yet this behavior was attention-getting, as if she were somehow left out. I think she had continued feelings of low self-esteem and, coupled with her feelings about her absentee father, made her create a ruckus around her so she could be noticed and loved. Had she been able to know how much she *was* loved, perhaps she could have concentrated on what she wanted in life instead of always feeling the need to fight each step of the way.

When the three kids worked at a local one-day event, the abuser was there building scaffolding for a stage. Cinnamon saw

him for the first time since the abuse ended over eight years earlier. Her gut knew it was Mark, but with so much time passing, he
couldn't have known her. She panicked and ran to her brothers,
who sequestered her in their shared car and called me. As her
original therapist had said, incidents would come up in her life
where the rush of the past would be overwhelming. This was the
first, and many others would manifest themselves in debilitating
migraine headaches.

Just gone out, back by
8:00. Have my phone if you
need me. I love you.
—Cinnamon

I need something because it is essential or very important. I need
my children to be safe and to have a roof over their head, food,
clothes to wear, and a good education to be used to contribute to
society. I need my children to have empathy for those who have
been injured or wronged. I need my children to become the best
they can be and strive to be even a bit better.

I don't need my children. I love my children unconditionally—well, most of the time—yet I don't always like them, the
people they might have momentarily become, or the life path
they have chosen. And I don't need to accept their choices.

I don't feel guilty about it, either.

During the child-rearing years, you give lectures on the
differences between right and wrong, your philosophy on life,
how best to avoid pregnancy at an early age, and how to get good
grades and create life options. They either listen, pretend to listen,

or don't listen. They text, tune out, or space out. The perfection of the art of eyeball rolling becomes paramount.

When they reach eighteen, whether or not they are ready, it's launch time—or, it used to be. Back in the day, we were standing in line at the DMV the morning of the sixteen-birthday celebration, chomping at the ignition switch. At high school graduation, we might not have known what we were doing, but we all knew it was far away from the high school practice field where we received our diplomas. Some kids knew from an early age and never wavered.

There were others whose toes tested the waters of the adult world and simply weren't ready.

Cinnamon never came back to live under the birth home roof, yet we never stopped supporting her. There was a car, the apartment, school—the normal—yet on a faraway continent. We didn't have the luxury of a visual sighting, the only real way you can tell how someone is doing. The goals were lofty, and I bought the entire package.

For the first few years, she went to school and worked. Then, there were "personality differences" with her immediate superiors. One was a lush, which was probably true, and the other stole all her ideas. That was, no doubt, true as well. Yet, when you are on a volunteer visa and not making enough money to get through on your own, your options are slim to none.

Queue the rename of the family financial institution to the Bank of Slim to None, echoing the dwindling career options. I couldn't let her dream go. Yes, I the parent attempted to keep her five-year-old childhood dream alive. I enabled her by supporting her for far too long, over eleven years. So even though she wasn't a boomerang child in the literal sense, she was definitely a strong pretender to that crown—and to the Mastercard.

It was my dream to actualize her dream. I wanted to support that altruistic world-changing lifestyle, so I endured endless lectures from one oldest son and endless lectures from the middle child fuck-up-made-good.

Her brothers wanted her to succeed as well—just to succeed on her own. She didn't have the tools or the necessary understanding that she could create her world by her choice, consciously or without thought. What she did, where she went, who she was with would guide her future. She would try, on her own terms. She entered a *National Geographic* Competition for New Ideas. Her idea was a community of native South Africans, working together to save animals and be self-sustaining. She didn't win the contest, yet I didn't know her dream would bring her to the brink of an unrelenting depression that would take years to overcome.

It's 10:50. Home safe and sound!
Love you
Sleep Well!
—*Cinnamon*

Happy to be chauffeured, she didn't drive until after she graduated from high school. The day of graduation, she mourned, "I'm the only senior who isn't driving to graduation." My reply was, "That has been a gift to me."

The time we spent in the mornings and afternoons would not have happened had she had a license. It was a precious time filled with memories of teenage anger, lack of sleep, and the general pissed-off behavior we as parents are subjected to for the better part of the tween and teenage years.

There was plenty to talk about: grades, grades, and more failing grades leading to a lack of life choices. My mantra for a good life is to always have a selection, but this had not been assimilated by the youngest member of the clan.

Most of the time, phone calls from your children's school are the result of misbehaving incidents. In our household, these weekly occurrences came to be known as the Mrs. Richmond phone calls.

In the beginning, I didn't feel as if I were being singled out for these special missives, yet, as time passed, I knew I was receiving more than my share. Oh, I knew other families were recipients of the dreaded calls from the front administrative office, yet these reminders of our less-than-perfect progeny weren't the topic of conversation on the playgrounds. I'd heard it all: failing grades, missing the deadline for a term paper, and poor classroom attitude as recorded by one instructor after another.

For parents of today's middle and high school students, there are more disturbing phone conversations due to more unsupervised time and open internet opportunities. I am lucky the calls had to do with missing homework and other more benign subjects.

The day she left for South Africa happened to be stormy, an electrical storm worthy of an All Hallows Eve haunted house nightmare. The last thing she told me was, "Dad's always handled the passports."

My reply was simple: "I hope you were watching."

It was a defining moment when the word "Dad" flowed effortlessly from the emotional stress of leaving home. Had she been hiding the desire to be loved, to be nurtured, and to dissolve the walls held so tightly for so many years? We took that moment for what each of us needed. It was a shame it took separation to unearth the basic human need to be love and be loved.

I walked away, turned a corner in the departure lounge area, and burst into tears. Not only was she traveling continents away, but I was trusting to the gods I wasn't sure I believed in to grant her a safe journey into the arms of someone I had only spoken to on the phone a few times. After all my research, the small training facility with under six students and run by a husband and wife team had been my choice for her eighteen-month schooling. Warm and engaging, this couple would welcome my youngest to their family, yet my capricious and cavalier attitude was a crumbling façade of fear and self-loathing. She was gone, and there wasn't a damn thing I could do about it.

The gods got her to her destination safely and into a great training program. Her roommate was a fifty-something woman from the United Kingdom who was starting her life over. Perfect! Or so I led myself to believe.

In retrospect, that year and a half was a reprieve. She seemed to be happy and to be growing up at the same time. Hindsight points to this time fondly as the problems had not begun to mount, somewhat like the humongous termite mounds she would proudly show me upon my first visit to her world when she would explain dung beetle behavior, scat differences, paw prints, the everlasting love elephants possess, night roaming rhinos, and all manner of creepy crawly creatures up to and including the majesty that is truly the king of the beasts.

I would be impressed with her knowledge and once again, I'd think, *Great, she is launched.* I thought she would be the first American field guide with a top award for field guiding or whatever it is called when you excel and win the prize. I never stopped believing that I had intellectually superior offspring. They were just guilty until proven innocent. Isn't that the way it should be?

Hi Mom and Dad
I'm fine, the dance was OK (it's currently 11:30)
I ♥ u
Sleep Well
—Cinnamon

I had shipped one off to Europe, one to Asia, and now the final one to Africa. Geographers claim there are seven continents. I had children covering at least three. How far away from me could they possibly desire to live?

I didn't dwell on the fact they were as far away as they actually were until an acquaintance said, "You showed them the world; what did you expect them to do, stay here?" There you go, my fault again. I can't seem to slide past that fact.

Folks who were attempting to be kind would talk about all the great places to visit. I would smile graciously. I was always gracious and would tell myself, yes someday, when the bank reverts to one beneficiary: me. The bank was still funding two out of three.

A part of Cinnamon's trail guide training was theory and the last third practical. Practical meant in the bush, in a guest lodge, waiting on guests and managing staff. She was always quite proficient in telling everyone what to do, so the staff management went well until someone did something to the contrary. Hey, that one landed close to home. The similarities are frighteningly uncanny.

She was placed in an upscale five-star lodge with well-traveled, well-off guests. She was the host, and, from what I hear, her tips were good, which indicated her adaptation to the needs, wants, and desires of others. A rite of maturity, right?

Well, one day, for some reason, her bosses began to crow, cackle, complain, and demand. Instead of placating (which would have been my suggestion, what with: a) living in a third world county; b) a very basic lack of work; and c) no work visa), she stood her ground and quit. I believe my children are guilty . . . remember? And I also believe the truth lies somewhere in the middle of two people's perspectives.

I hear this mantra from her age group: "Well, it wasn't what I wanted to do," or "It was too much work."

What the bloody hell? It's a phenomenon most relevant to millennials. They don't have the same need for job security, opting to move on when they aren't happy, fulfilled, excited, challenged, or paid according to their sense of importance. I remember my mother saying to me, "Never quit a job before you have the next one lined up."

I worked in college at the State Highway Department, walking from one building to the next delivering paperwork. Walking, walking, walking, and delivering the same work orders day after day. That department made stop signs. Day after day, stop signs.

An older gentleman who was my immediate superior retired while I was still working there. They actually gave him a gold watch. I thought that was just stuff from television shows, but no, it was real. I knew I had to get out of there. There were a couple of shining moments at my first real job: nice, honest people; a cute man to date for a while; and the biggest perk— an unexpected place to clean. Do you remember a time before self-cleaning ovens? I moved out of my apartment and had a nasty stove to clean. The parts of the oven were removable, so off to work I took them, to be dipped clean in something they used to clean stop signs. I was a happy housekeeper. That being the very few saving graces to that position, I knew I could check off having an entry-level position in the sign department at the local state level from my life's work. This is how it used to be done, one job at a time. You found out what you liked and what you couldn't abide.

I'm home.
Its 11:00
Dinner with a friend at Denny's . . . eyes tonight were definitely bigger than stomach (see fridge for leftovers)

Hi! It is 12:15
Sorry so late.
Ran into an old friend from school and had dinner with him.
Sleep well
—Cinnamon

Well, any parent worth their investigative talents knows that teenage dinners do not last until midnight. We all remember, because we tried the same lies when we were their age.

White lies are important to:

a) Not get in trouble.
b) Prevent our parents from worrying about us.
and
c) Do things that otherwise would not be allowed!

I lied to my mother until the day she died at ninety-nine years old. I didn't want her to think I was not as perfect as she had hoped.

Yet, I knew the truth. She probably did, too.

I knew some truths with Cinnamon; she was testing limits. At seventeen and secretly seeing a nineteen-year-old, would she have the sense to remember the core of her upbringing? What was I afraid of the most in my midnight thoughts? Would her zeal create a strong, independent, and fierce woman, confident to navigate a patriarchal society with gusto and succeed, not merely because she is a woman, but because she had whatever it takes to honestly make a statement in this world? Or would hurt bring up abandonment from her father and abuse issues just under the skin surface? I was dancing on a thin line, and we made a contract. On the advice of her therapist, she could see the secret boyfriend in public but not at his apartment. This did not go over well.

Sometimes it's better not to know, yet I wanted to know—not about the sordid details of white lies, but if I was a good enough mother to save her from life and its harshest lessons. Had I given enough, even when I thought I had given everything? How could I have done more to protect her from the world of woeful regrets? My heart ached for a moment when I would get the pat on the back and hear, "Don't worry, you did just fine." I wonder if that time will ever come.

Thank you for finding my list—
sunglasses and a T-shirt for Becky.
Good time back at school.

Saw lots of old friends and a couple of teachers and showed lots of my photos. Hung with Laura for about an hour. Home at 11:00.
Love you
—Cinnamon

First time home from life with the wild bush babies and an empty suitcase, there were stories from the bush and a zest for life I hadn't seen. She was really alive. It was very exciting to hear the subtle change in the lilt of her accent and see the incredible photos. It was a good time, yet as we all know, the good doesn't last.

She went to university to learn the language that Westerners know as "click," one of the official languages of over 7.6 million people, most commonly known as Xhosa. It is a Nguni Bantu language with click consonants ("Xhosa" begins with a click), one of the official languages of South Africa and spoken by about 18 percent of the South African population. The Bantu languages are a very large group, belonging to the Benue-Congo family of the Niger-Congo phylum, which comprises between 250 to 500 members spread over most of sub-Saharan Africa. They are spoken by nearly one-third of the population of the continent, approximately 330 million people. Like most other Bantu languages, Xhosa is a tonal language: the same sequence of consonants and vowels can have different meanings, depending on intonation. Xhosa has two tones: high and low.

The story has been told of the American tourist, sitting in a café or at an event in a foreign country, where people speak languages other than English. The locals are talking freely about the foreigner's dress, loud and obnoxious manner of speaking, or otherwise less-than-stellar observations, only to have

the cool visitor turn and ask a question in the fluent voice of
the native tongue. The embarrassed locals shrink away while
the learned speaker smiles inwardly at his feigned superiority.
These types of stories abound from Vietnamese nail salons to the
Champs-Élysée. It must have been something to witness when
the pale-skinned Californian girl busted the Xhosa group in their
own language. I don't know why she couldn't have learned French
or Spanish or Mandarin, except that the dream of owning a farm
and hiring locals required a knowledge of their native tongue.
She hadn't dreamed of the French Rivera or bustling Shanghai,
so her choice wasn't a surprise.

Cinnamon would become a mother herself, content with
a life as far away from her upbringing as you could imagine. At
first, I railed at what looked to be abject poverty with no visible
way out. While it still looks like that to me, I have let go. Will I
be there if it fails? Of course. Yet, with great personal resolve, I
recognize that I have zero control over who she is, how she raises
her family, or the choices she makes. In the inimitable words of a
much-loved family therapist, "With adult children, you get three
choices; wait, watch, and pray."

Acknowledgments

The goal of this writing comes from a passionate belief that my story can inspire women to succeed when the outlook is bleak and hopeless. Women have an incredible, singular force of will for survival and are indomitable.

My incentive for writing this book comes from a few swift kicks in the ass, the dread of the unfinished, the abject horror of those portrayed, the demise of a long friendship due to creative differences, and other normal, life-threatening issues found in life.

Thanks to MMC for the initial boot and her introduction to Brooke, who guided with empathy and a firm hand; my children, who cringed with each edit; and my husband, who said, "Just keep writing." There were those who encouraged me through my bouts of insecurity: Marcia, Cindy, and Amy. Leslie showered me with books about writing and weekly motivational emojis. There were many unknown names and forgotten faces on airplanes, in waiting rooms, and in hotel lobbies who were curious about the woman hunched over a computer screen, typing furiously while carrying on animated conversations with imaginary characters. I tested the concept on them and received candid feedback while they slowly backed away, looking for the nearest exit route.

These truths are mine, brought to life by memories on scraps of paper. Recollections are not always shared agreements by all parties in attendance, and my musings are dotted with motherly guilt, pride, and seared images of pretend horrors and real-life chaos.

Postscript

Women marry, divorce, raise their children, remarry, and live their lives. The circumstances might be more humorous, sad, silly, crazy, or terrifying, but the story is the same.

Why write the story?

Barring death and destruction, my story, like theirs, like yours, will work out. It won't work out exactly as desired, but it will work out. You will live through it. There will be terrific memories, and there will be memories better left alone. You and I did the best we could with the tools we had at the time.

It's time to let go of any guilt or misconceptions about how things could have turned out had we only known.

I know I was blessed to have kept all those silly pieces of paper under the door after midnight, then and now.

About the Author

Though born in St. Joseph, Michigan, a beach town on Lake Michigan, Carol Richmond spent years of winters bouncing between Florida, Louisiana, Texas, and Mississippi. She settled in California and lived forty years on the central coast of California until her husband's early retirement precipitated the move to a farm, purchased in 2005, on an island in the middle of the Pacific Ocean. Richmond now divides her time between the farm and the Monterey peninsula. The island serves as a creative respite, cooking and baking retreat, and writing solitude; the Mainland madness feeds her joy imbuing children with a love of ballet and theatre. She continues to nurture her first passion, the performing arts, as the director of a business with a sixty-five-year history of excellence. The three children portrayed in this memoir live as far away from her as possible yet are currently all speaking to each other . . . for now.

Author Photo © Robert Ellis Photography

Selected Titles From She Writes Press

She Writes Press is an independent publishing company founded to serve women writers everywhere. Visit us at www.shewritespress.com.

The Buddha at My Table: How I Found Peace in Betrayal and Divorce by Tammy Letherer. $16.95, On a Tuesday night, just before Christmas, after he had put their three children in bed, Tammy Letherer's husband shattered her world and destroyed every assumption she'd ever made about love, friendship, and faithfulness. In the aftermath of this betrayal, however, she finds unexpected blessings—and, ultimately, the path to freedom.

Warrior Mother: A Memoir of Fierce Love, Unbearable Loss, and Rituals that Heal by Sheila K. Collins, PhD. $16.95, 978-1-938314-46-9. The story of the lengths one mother goes to when two of her three adult children are diagnosed with potentially terminal diseases.

Breathe: A Memoir of Motherhood, Grief, and Family Conflict by Kelly Kittel. $16.95, 978-1-938314-78-0. A mother's heartbreaking account of losing two sons in the span of nine months—and learning, despite all the obstacles in her way, to find joy in life again.

Loveyoubye: Holding Fast, Letting Go, And Then There's The Dog by Rossandra White. $16.95, 978-1-938314-50-6. A soul-searching memoir detailing the painful, but ultimately liberating, disintegration of a twenty-five-year marriage.

The Full Catastrophe: A Memoir by Karen Elizabeth Lee. $16.95, 978-1-63152-024-2. The story of a well educated, professional woman who, after marrying the wrong kind of man—twice—finally resurrects her life.

Not Exactly Love: A Memoir by Betty Hafner. $16.95, 978-1-63152-149-2. At twenty-five Betty Hafner, thought she'd found the man to make her dream of a family and cozy home come true—but after they married, his rages turned the dream into a nightmare, and Betty had to decide: stay with the man she loved, or find a way to leave?